CHASING STEAM ON SHED

1956~1968

Peter Hands

Barbryn Press Limited

To my wife Annette, and children Sarah and Stephen, with all my love and everlasting thanks for their patience.

Acknowledgements

I would especially like to thank my good friend Barry Homer, not only for the years we shared together on the many shed trips, but also for reminding me of some events which otherwise I might have overlooked.

My thanks also to Bryan Holden for his practical advice and constant encouragement in the preparation of both this book and my 'What Happened to Steam' series.

Also to Harold Parsons and Dick Potts for assisting in the final presentation of the manuscript.

And last, but not least, to Gary Evans for his apt cartoons which have captured the mood of the moment far better than any words of mine can describe.

First published in 1982 by Barbryn Press Limited

ISBN 0 906160 030

Printed in Great Britain by Streetly Printing (Birmingham) Limited for Barbryn Press Limited, 61 Cornwall Street, Birmingham B2 2EB.

Design & artwork production Barbryn Press Limited, Birmingham.

Introduction

My story begins in 1956 when almost 18,000 steam locomotives were to be seen up and down the country and many rail fans devoted their young lives to seeing as many of them as possible. In some ways it was perhaps sheer madness, and in many people's eyes a waste of time and money, but given those days all over again, I and many others like me would do exactly the same.

Nowadays, thanks to thriving preservation movements, thousands of people of both sexes and of all ages can visit the many splendidly preserved railways and steam centres and enjoy themselves to the full, albeit during the summer months, and generally in comfort.

How different things were twenty-five years ago! Now many of today's fathers were then, like myself, looking at, and searching for steam locomotives in entirely different circumstances. I never dreamed in 1961 that ten years later I would be at some of the old Motive Power Depots, looking at steam locomotives alongside ladies with children in prams, and with sales stands and sideshows for extra entertainment. No offence, ladies; but when steam ruled the rails, railway enthusiasm was certainly a male dominated preserve!

In this retrospective journey I have recalled my experiences as a schoolboy on local railway stations, further afield by rail, and on to joining some railway societies. I have also described some of the many hazards and pitfalls (literally!) which faced ardent spotters during unofficial shed visits.

I hope that the details of locomotives seen and the places and sheds covered, together with photographs, will bring back happy memories to other railway fans, many of whom I knew and travelled with.

PETER HANDS
Solihull
January 1982

Two ex-LMS Class 8F 2-8-0s Nos 48702 and 48720 await their inevitable fate after closure of 9K Bolton. 27 July 1968.

Contents

'TRAIN-SPOTTERS... GENERALLY A DISHEVELLED AND SORRY LOOKING LOT..

The Enthusiast

Nowadays the hobby of railways has become entirely respectable and steam enthusiasts are of both sexes, all ages and from many different levels of society. Most are generally better dressed and equipped than their predecessors of some twenty-five years ago.

Even so, the more fanatical elements can be recognised as being festooned with several cameras of both the still and movie variety and tape recorders fitted with a variety of microphones. In extreme cases the amount of equipment can rival even that of the marines and commandos out on manoeuvres.

On the steam hauled specials of today there is always a cadre of these fellows crowding the windows of the first two or three carriages, each one of them generally attired in a standard dress of leather jacket, balaclava helmet and goggles.

However, the vast majority of these fans do not travel on the specials but spend all day pursuing them for photographic reasons. Once the train has passed by their cameras, they then attempt to break the world sprint record in getting back to their cars in a frantic effort to be first off the mark and en route for the next location down the line. One of the days I fully expect to read in a newspaper of a four way collision at a remote crossroads, somewhat akin to what happened to Inspector Clousseau in one of the 'Pink Panther' films!

But things were very different in the 1950s and 1960s when thousands of steam engines abounded from Penzance to Wick. In those days enthusiasts of all ages were called trainspotters and were generally looked down upon with distaste by the public at large. The main group of spotters were aged between ten and twenty years of age but their numbers thinned out as they grew older and moved on to other pursuits.

Trainspotters' standard dress consisted of either short or nearly long trousers which generally had creases everywhere instead of in the right places, shoes invariably covered in mud, ashes or dust — or a combination of all three — duffle coat or macintosh and a duffle bag or haversack containing a variety of curled up sandwiches or rolls and biscuits. Usually, by the end of a hard day's trainspotting these bags contained a mixture of bits of sandwich filling, bananas which had gone black and had been squashed, and other unsavoury items. Coat pockets were stuffed with sweets, notebooks, pens, pencils and the inevitable well-worn locoshed book.

It is easy, therefore, to understand why members of the public were reluctant to mingle with these apparently cast out members of society. We were generally a dishevelled and sorry looking lot, but the main reason for being so ill-dressed was because, in many cases, especially with the older boys, spare cash was spent on rail trips rather than buying clothes. To spend money on clothes was considered a last resort, to be done only when the sole of a shoe fell off or a trouser fly zip would no longer do up. How our parents must have despaired of ever getting us to look smart!

The hobby of trainspotting also seemed to attract some of the poorer elements of the schoolboy age group; poor not just in financial terms but physical as well: for example, the ones who were no good at cricket, football and rugby, or were too shy to go out with girls — the cast offs: little fat boys described as "Toby Jugs" or contrastingly tall thin boys with large ears, most with spotty faces and some with buck teeth. To prove that I mean no offence to these lads I was the small and thin one with large ears.

Many were equipped with grotesque National Health glasses, and even with these they had great difficulty in seeing the numbers of engines even from a short distance. They were the types who claimed to have seen Western and Southern Region engines at stations like York, for instance. Other types used to fudge the numbers that they ruled in their spotting books, that is to say they pretended to have seen engines which they had not seen. Woe betide anyone who was caught actually doing so: he would be scorned and ridiculed to the extent that he would have to go into exile.

Having thus described the mannerisms and general appearance of the average trainspotter, one can well understand the misgivings and doubts towards them of the public at large. How tiresome it must have been for travellers entering mainline stations to be confronted by garrulous bands of thirty or more spotters brandishing sandwiches and spotting books and racing up and down the platform at the arrival and departure of every train. No wonder my wife's mother warned her to stay away from us, "There's something wrong with them," she said. Little did she know at the time the fate awaiting her daughter in later years!

The Early Years
1956-1958

Small Beginnings

When railway enthusiasts get together for the first time an invariable question is, "How and when did you get interested in railways and, in particular, steam locomotives?" My first conscious memory is at a very early age being held over a railway bridge by my father just as a steam engine passed underneath. I remember being terrified, but it obviously did not have a lasting effect.

My enthusiasm for steam started in the spring of 1956 when as a ten year old a school pal asked me to go to Solihull station on the Birmingham-Paddington main line, just for something to do. I remember the first three steam engines I saw, all ex GWR — 2-6-2T No 4111, No 6028 *King George VI* and No 6910 *Gossington Hall.* Nos 4111 and 6910 survived into the last year of steam on the Western region — 1965.

From then on I virtually lived at Solihull Station in my spare time until I was allowed to venture further afield. In those days there were four tracks and the line was extremely busy. All through the summer I enjoyed seeing those magnificent green liveried locomotives at the head of such expresses as the "Cambrian Coast Express," and the "Inter-City". "Castles," "Counties," "Kings," "Granges," "Halls" abounded on this route, along with the many other ex GWR types on trains to Birkenhead, London and the south coast towns. What a pity that British Railways did away with the lovely livery of chocolate and cream on their coaches. They were a fabulous sight.

At the very beginning of my trainspotting days I knew only of the ABC book of Western Region locos which included the BR standards, so that when an ex LMS engine passed through Solihull and I was unable to find it in my book, I dismissed it on the grounds that it was of "foreign" origin.

During the autumn of 1956 I was allowed to go to Birmingham (Snow Hill), travelling in the now defunct compartment suburban stock. At the time it was quite a terrifying ordeal to go on such a journey as this on one's own at ten years of age, travelling to the big city past huge factories and stations I had never heard of. After what seemed an eternity (twenty minutes!) the train entered the cavernous tunnel by Birmingham (Moor Street) and emerged into Snow Hill Station. What a fabulous place it was. I spent many a happy day at this station.

Stafford

During the winter months of 1956/57 I ceased trainspotting, and the spring of 1957 brought me my first real opportunity to discover that there was another world of railways outside the limits of the Western region. I went with my family on holiday to Rhyl by train from Birmingham (New

Street), a drab and confusing place, but infinitely more preferable to the concrete monstrosity that is New Street today. Journeying to Rhyl, I soon discovered that LMS engines were not 'foreign' after all, and a whole new avenue for spotting began to open up.

We changed trains at Stafford and I remember two locomotives: "Royal Scot" No 46161 *King's Own* storming through on an up express, and our own train engine "Coronation" No 46253 *City of St. Albans.* Needless to say, I soon had in my possession an ABC book on ex LMS locos.

Throughout the summer of 1957 many Saturdays were spent at Stafford. The return half fare from Birmingham was about 2s 10d (roughly 14p!). How magical those days were, with a steady stream of "Patriots", "Jubilees", "Scots", "Princesses", "Coronations" and "Britannias". The named trains they hauled had their own kind of magic too: "Royal Scot", "Mid-Day Scot", "Comet", "Manxman", "Mancunian" and "Red Rose", to name but a few. The only diesels to be seen were Nos 10000/1 and 10201-3 (how soon this was to change).

Apart from being an extremely busy station on the West Coast main line, Stafford was also a junction for the lines from Birmingham and Shrewsbury. It had the added advantage of having a steam shed adjacent to it and during the course of the day many engines could be observed working on and off the depot.

4-6-0 No 1006 County of Cornwall *83D Laira (Plymouth) 29 April 1962*

I was allowed to go to Stafford providing I arrived home in the early evening, but on one occasion the train I normally caught failed to arrive and I was stranded well beyond the time I should have been home. Naturally my parents were worried sick and despite being told the truth they believed I had stayed at Stafford deliberately, and I was banned from going there. I obeyed my parents to the letter for a short while but the lure of those magnificent engines soon drew me back again.

I got away with this deception for some time, implying that I never strayed beyond Wolverhampton, but one day I let slip that I had 'copped' a certain "Coronation" loco on the "Royal Scot", to which the reply came back rather sourly, "The Royal Scot doesn't go through Wolverhampton". However, after this I was allowed officially to continue at Stafford with my hobby.

Nostalgia prompts me to mention one or two unusual aspects and items of interest about this station. There were two signals on the through lines which had nicknames, one on the up fast being a huge sooty semaphore known as "Big Ben" and a colour signal on the down line known appropriately as "Little Ben". Another feature was a bell which used to ring continuously (I believe still in use) heralding the approach of a through express.

Back in 1957 it was not unusual to see pigeon trains and Stafford was a starting point for races. Several vans would be stabled in one of the bay platforms and the birds would be released in the afternoon. On one occasion a bird refused to join the race and, after several sorties, decided that one of the rails on the up main line was a good place for a stroll, despite an express being signalled. The express came roaring into sight and despite the cacophony of noise from the locomotive, vibrating rails and the attentions of waiting passengers, the bird stubbornly refused to fly off. Seconds later it lost out in the battle of wills as it disappeared under the leading wheels of "Jubilee" No 45588 *Kashmir,* as it hurtled southwards.

Whilst on the subject of birds, I remember "Britannia" No 70045 *Lord Rowallan* storming southwards on the "Irish Mail" with a seagull spread-eagled on the smokebox, and later in the day the same loco returned northbound with the bird still in position.

At Stafford I learnt that it was better, at large stations, to try and trainspot on your own rather than in a crowd, for occasionally the station staff would swoop on spotters and escort them from the station. Being included on these round-ups often meant the difference between spotting in relative comfort under cover, or spending an uncomfortable day peeping over bridges on tip-toe with nowhere to sit, usually in the rain.

Shirley

Another station I visited regularly from 1957 was Shirley on the North Warwickshire line from Snow Hill to Gloucester. Summer Saturday evenings produced a procession of holiday trains returning from the West Country. Although this line lacked the glamour of others, many rare engines from far away depots could be spotted. These heavy trains were often double-headed and included "Counties", "Castles", "Halls" and "Granges" from such places as Bristol, Exeter, Plymouth and Swansea — the quality ones not often seen in the Birmingham area. Sadly the line now terminates at Stratford-upon-Avon and is sparsely used south of Shirley.

Tamworth

1957 passed by and again I went into winter hibernation, saving my pennies for the warmer months of 1958 during which I was to add Tamworth to my Saturday outings. The main attraction here was the meeting of the West Coast main line (low level) and the Midland line (high level) from Bristol-Newcastle. Consequently, the place was besieged by spotters on Saturdays and the station staff were fully prepared for this onslaught. As fast as spotters arrived on early trains from Birmingham and other places they were escorted to the exits.

Forbidden the station, the spotters gathered in a field situated between the two main lines and the River Anker. As trains passed by, passengers used to stare and shake their heads in disbelief at the sight of hundreds of assorted enthusiasts crammed into a small corner of the field, jockeying for the best positions.

A rotten trick frequently performed by train crews on the high level was to cover up the cabside number as they passed by. Unless the loco was named or you caught a quick glimpse of the smokebox number, all you could do was stand there in frustration.

During the late afternoon the majority of spotters returned from whence they came, much to the relief of the station staff. Both lines are still busy today but most of the spotters are gone and the field is now a residential caravan site.

One story from a friend who used to be a fireman at Saltley referred to a set of water troughs situated a few miles to the Derby side of the high level station. On the odd occasion a goggle-bedecked spotter would be seen leaning out of a window nearest to the locomotive, and for many a train crew it was beyond temptation to let the odd gallon of water flow out of the tender top whilst on the troughs. No doubt the recipient was not quite so impressed by the idea!

As at Stafford some of the Tamworth signals were nick-named. Two that come to mind, situated on the low level, were “Clanger” and “Baby Clanger”, although I have no idea of their origins.

Whilst reminiscing about relationships between railway staff and spotters, I always found in the main, providing the spotters behaved themselves, they were usually left alone. In my experience I only came across two stations which were notorious for ejecting spotters, One, already mentioned was Tamworth, the other being Birmingham (New Street). The prime spot at this station was the London end where the Midland and LNW lines converged closely between platforms 6 and 7. Spotters would be mostly unmolested, but from time to time the railway police would have a purge and we would be dispersed by hard-faced officers who gave the impression of a job easily done. However, ardent rail fans, like bad pennies, would keep turning up. We would simply reassemble at the Wolverhampton end only to be moved on yet again. This would go on alternatively until, at the end of a couple of hours, the police gave it up as a bad job.

Steam Sheds

During 1958 I took my first tentative steps to gain access to the inside of steam sheds. My first attempts were at 84E Tyseley, all ending in miserable failure a few yards from the gateman. Eventually I was introduced to the 'back' entrance, a well trodden path across wasteland, along a cleverly constructed 'bridge' of tree trunks and various bric-a-brac over a stream and into the depot, out of sight of the gatekeeper. Invariably I was caught, ticked off and escorted off the premises but the lure of these vast cathedrals of steam was too much to resist despite the various threats from irate foreman and the like. Over the years it became a cat and mouse game, with a mountain of excuses as to why you were in the depots, most of which were held in total disbelief by the shed staff. I only came near to 'prosecution for trespass' once. (described later).

The second depot I 'bunked' (spotters jargon for unofficial shed visits) was 84A Wolverhampton (Stafford Road). I always walked the distance from one of the main stations along a canal to the shed. My main memory of this walk was the state of the canal, which looked as if the water consisted of black treacle. I dread to think how many toxic substances had been introduced to it over the years.

Access to the shed was easy from this side as the tow-path was adjacent to the coaling plant and yard area. Having braved the distance from under the viaduct carrying the Wolverhampton-Stafford line to the running shed, it was invariably safe. However, being inexperienced, I often jumped at shadows, imagining all types of pursuers, so that my nerve would crack halfway round, and I would retreat to the safety of the towpath — I had a lot to learn!

Scotland

In the late summer of 1958 I had the opportunity of a holiday with an aunt at Aberfoyle, north of Glasgow. Having previously been no further than Crewe, my imagination ran riot. I studied a map and my mouth drooled at the prospect, for there were no less than eighteen steam sheds to be passed on route. Apart from the obvious delights of Shap and Beattock was the crossing of the Scottish border for the first time, passing through unheard of and now almost forgotten railway stations like Ecclefechan, Netherclough and Elvanfoot.

I had been saving my pocket money towards this holiday and eventually the day of departure arrived and, with a name and address tag around my neck, I was ready for the off. By this time I had spotted most of the English-based named passenger locos on the West Coast route of the LMR but had not seen any of the Scottish ones. There was an engine change at Crewe and lo-and-behold — my first Scottish cop — "Britannia" No 70052 *Firth of Tay,* of Polmadie — magic!

The entire journey from Crewe was spent standing, my head continuously out of an open window, so that when I arrived in Glasgow I was as black as the ace of spades. Highlights of the journey included pounding up Shap and Beattock, both with the aid of a banking engine. I saw my first "Clans" and copped a bagful of Scottish "Royal Scots" and "Coronations" on the journey. Of these Scottish rarities, it was the concensus of opinion in Birmingham amongst the spotters that Nos 46102 *Black Watch* and 46220 *Coronation* were the rarest, but during this journey north I saw neither of them.

At Aberfoyle there was unfortunately no railway, so for three enjoyable but frustrating weeks I saw no steam, except on a day trip to Edinburgh when I was able to persuade my aunt to let me go to Waverley station for an hour or so, where for the first time I was able to spot ER locos in any numbers. My first A4 cop was No 60030 *Golden Fleece* on the down "Elizabethan", followed by No 60011 *Empire of India* with various other "Pacifics" and "Shires" to be seen. How I wish I could have stayed for a complete day.

The end of the holiday arrived and whereas I suppose most people would be sad and miserable on the journey home, I had the prospect of a 300 miles trainspotting journey to look forward too. I did, however, get off to a bad start at Glasgow (Central). The place was a hive of activity with all types of locos buzzing in and out and in my excitement I broke my pencil and neither my aunt nor uncle had a replacement. This was a lesson to be learned; never go spotting with only one writing implement. I spent many a long minute waiting in frustration, missing many potential cops before a replacement was purchased, mostly due to adults not understanding the crisis at hand.

Whilst waiting for the Birmingham train I had a walk to the end of the platform and there to my surprise and pleasure was "Coronation" No 46220 *Coronation* herself at the head of the up "Royal Scot" — what a cop! Little did I realise but this engine was only a few days off being transferred to Crewe and so becoming commonplace throughout my usual haunts.

I was rather disappointed to find that my own train engine was the familiar "Coronation" No 46228 *Duchess of Rutland* from Crewe. The journey home passed all too soon, but I had spotted many hundreds of steam engines including many of my remaining named LMR types, and seen many rarities in the shape of Caledonians and some LNER locos, adding up to a most fruitful journey.

After a few more visits to Stafford and Tamworth, 1958 came to an end and once again I went into winter hibernation.

2-6-0 N Class No 31855. 83H Friary (Plymouth). 29 April 1962

2-6-2T's Nos 5531 & 4564. 83E St Blazey. 29 April 1962

Full Steam on Shed

1959-1960

1959 provided a marked increase in journeys to different venues. The feelings of an avid trainspotter are difficult to relate to someone who does not understand the motives behind the urge to travel. I felt I had to go beyond the last station I had previously been to, and in all different directions, to find out what lay beyond. Apart from local stations and Stafford and Tamworth, the most distant locations of Paddington, Gloucester, Swindon, Hereford, Bristol and the north of Scotland were to be my venues.

Paddington

In the early spring of this year I had my first day trip to Paddington. By this time I had seen all of the "Kings" with the exception of those based at Laira (Plymouth). I assume a spotter in Plymouth had equally as hard a time to cop Wolverhampton-based engines in his area. On this first visit I polished off Nos 6004/10/11/17/21/25 and 6027, leaving only Nos 6026 *King John* and 6029 *King Edward VIII* to be spotted. I also saw many of the remaining named locos of the Western that I still needed and many of the Cardiff (Canton) based "Britannias". My one big regret was not even to attempt visits to any of the other London termini, whilst at Paddington. Indeed, apart from Paddington, Waterloo was the only other London station where I saw steam. One of those wasted opportunities that doesn't seem important at the time, but certainly are later on.

I made the mistake of trainspotting on two consecutive Saturdays at Paddington and many of the engines I had copped on my first visit were there again on more or less the same workings. This taught me to vary my long distance venues as much as possible. Nevertheless, I enjoyed myself at Paddington and loved some of the titles of the named trains — "Merchant Venturer", "Royal Duchy", "Cathedrals", "Mayflower" and of course the 'premier' one "The Cornish Riviera". It was here that I saw my first new mainline diesels — "Warships" Nos D601/2/4 and D801-4, but they were so insignificant in numbers compared to steam that I did not realise how quickly they would replace steam in the next few years.

Gloucester and Swindon

My next trip was to Gloucester and Swindon, the only occasion I was to travel behind steam up Sapperton Bank, in the shape of "Castle" No 5017 *The Gloucestershire Regiment 28th, 61st,* piloted by 2-6-2T No 5184. I boarded the train at Gloucester and as it was raining heavily I decided to sit down for a change and got myself comfortably seated by a window. The train had come from Cheltenham and prior to leaving Gloucester the compartment became full. I did not mind as I had positioned myself so that I would be facing the direction of travel; ideal for spotting, or so I thought.

As the train started to move I thought to my horror that I was on the wrong one, for it went off in the opposite direction to that expected. In my ignorance I had not realised that the train reversed at Gloucester. Making myself suitably sorry-looking, I grovelled to a lady opposite and explained my predicament. Although she looked at me as if I was quite mad, she agreed to change places. This was another lesson to be learned prior to a spotting trip — to find out not only where you are going but which way!

Although I enjoyed myself at Swindon it was exasperating to see so many steam engines in and around the vicinity of the works, as it was impossible to see the numbers on them. Even more annoying was the fact that many were in for scrapping and could never be spotted again. The return journey to Gloucester was on a multiple unit, the first of many occasions over the years to come when, surrounded by steam hauled trains, mine would be diesel.

Bristol

During May 1959 I went on a day excursion from Birmingham (Snow Hill) to Bristol, hauled in both directions by "Hall" 4-6-0 No 5912 *Queen's Hall* of Tyseley. It was on this trip that I met a fellow spotter, Barry Homer, who was to become a life-long friend and associate with whom I was to spend many a harrowing yet humorous trip, trainspotting in future years by all modes of transport. We had an excellent day spotting at Bristol, with many engines 'copped'. What I did not know at the time was that it would be the only time I would see Bath Road shed full of steam.

BR Class 4 4-6-0 No 75052. Railway Enthusiasts Club visit to 1A Willesden. 20 May 1962

57XX Class 0-6-0 PT No 9768 drifts through Birmingham (Snow Hill) on a pick-up freight. 2 July 1962

LMS Class 5 4-6-0 No 44765 at Birmingham (New Street) with empty stock from Crewe. Loco fitted with double chimney. 8 July 1962

Scotland Again

Moving on to late August, I was once again fortunate enough to go and stay with my aunt; this time for three weeks, in a hotel south of Aviemore. Like the previous year I set off with a name and address tag around my neck, drooling at the prospect of a twelve hour spotting journey. I had to change trains at Crewe to one bound for Perth and to my delight it was one of my last few remaining "Royal Scots" No 46121 *Highland Light Infantry, City of Glasgow Regiment* of Polmadie which was to be the train engine. I spent most of the journey, as usual, with my head stuck out of a window. When the train branched off at Motherwell I was on new territory again. Passing Motherwell shed, which was packed with steam, for some strange reason I became obsessed with noting as many of the numbers of the small diesel shunters which were present, mostly of the D27 series as I had not seen any before and consequently the shed was passed before I realised what I was doing. On arrival at Perth I had to change again for a train to Inverness and whilst waiting I walked up the platform to have another look at 46121. There to my surprise was the elusive "Royal Scot" No 46102 *Black Watch* — a real 'catch'. Unbeknown to myself there had been a loco change at Carlisle and not only did I cop *Black Watch* but I had also had a run behind her, a real triumph!

Eventually I arrived at Aviemore and found that the hotel I was staying at was no more than a stone's throw from the main line, albeit single track.

V3 Class 2-6-2T No 67636, then the only active steam loco on 52C Blaydon. 6 April 1963

Every morning, with the possible exception of a Sunday, the "Royal Highlander" would storm past on the last leg of its long run from Euston. This heavy train would either be powered by two ex LMS "Black 5s" or a "Black 5" and a BR Class 5. These locos were the mainstay of this route, but there was plenty of activity to be seen concerning Caledonian locos including the smart-looking 4-4-0s. The only diesels to be seen were a few small shunters based at Inverness.

Whilst at Aviemore I obtained a railrover ticket for the area and did several trips to Inverness either via the main line and over Slochd summit or via the now long closed line over Dava Moor and Forres. On one such trip, I could not resist the temptation to have a go at bunking Inverness shed, quite a feat at the time considering I had been around only Tyseley and Wolverhampton (Stafford Road) up to now. It was an unusual depot in that it was a full roundhouse but only partially covered, like the continental ones.

Having successfully negotiated most of the shed without mishap, I then experienced one of those minor accidents which befell intrepid rail fans from time to time. Whilst gazing into the cab of a Caledonian 4-4-0, I stepped backwards in an effort to gain a better view and all but fell into a manhole filled with water. I managed to regain my balance in time but at the expense of getting one leg of my trousers, my shoe and a sock soaking wet. To make matters worse I was then apprehended by the shed foreman who compelled me to follow him to his office. When he found out how old I was and where I had come from, I received only a mild rebuke for being in the shed. He pointed out that if I insisted on going round steam sheds without permission I should at the very least watch where I was going. I was then permitted to dry out in front of a stove, after which he took me round the shed.

Looking back over the years, on all the shed visits around Scotland, I must say I found nothing but politeness from foremen and shedmasters who often went out of their way to assist. This is more than could be said of most of their kind south of the border.

The holiday once again passed all too quickly before starting the long journey home to Birmingham. Only three particular locos stick out in my mind on this return journey. A1 No 60145 *St. Mungo* at Perth at the head of an express, I was pulled from Perth to Carlisle by "Clan" No 72003 *Clan Fraser* and from Carlisle to Crewe by rebuilt "Patriot" No 45512 *Bunsen* of Crewe (North). This turned out to by my last visit to Scotland for three years by which time many of the expresses would be in the hands of main line diesels.

The end of the summer service in 1959 heralded the end of regular visits to Stafford and Tamworth and the winter proved to be the last in hibernation from trainspotting over the colder months.

1960

Although visits to local stations continued, as they did for many years to come, the search was on to find ways of spending a day at different locations in an attempt to see the remaining named locos of the Western and London Midland Regions, all within the limits of my spending power which was now financed by a paper round. By 1960 the named engines I needed from the WR were based mainly at depots in the West Country and in South and West Wales. From the LMR I was down to a handful of namers from Carlisle (Kingmoor), Kentish Town and Leicester, mostly "Jubilees". Likewise, I also needed a few "Jubilees", "Royal Scots" and "Coronations" from the North Eastern and Scottish Regions. I had seen very few named engines LNER-wise and none at all off the Southern. Indeed, the only Southern I had seen at all were a few 2-6-0s on shed at Cheltenham, these having worked over the old MSWJR system from Andover.

Derby

My first day out in 1960 was to Derby where I hoped to spot some of the ex WR "Britannias" which had not long been transferred to the Midland division from Cardiff (Canton). It was an extremely cold February day, most uncomfortable when standing for long periods. It was worth it though, as I was able to cop two of the "Britannias" Nos 70015 *Apollo* and 70017 *Arrow,* leaving me only No 70021 *Morning Star* to cop from the WR batch. I remember vividly the sad lines of condemned "Compounds", elderly tanks and freight engines standing forlornly in every available siding. I also had my first look at the brand new "Peaks", No D1 *Scafell Pike* amongst them and also at some of the 'handsome' Metrovicks! Like at Paddington in 1959, these diesels were so insignificant in numbers to pose any threats to steam.

A3 Class 4-6-2 Flying Scotsman *on its first public outing in private ownership Birmingham (Snow Hill). 20 April 1963*

4-6-0 No 5057 Earl Waldegrave *in steam. 82C Swindon. 28 April 1963*

4-6-2 No 34094 Mortehoe. *With a Warwickshire Railway Society special from Birmingham (New Street). 36A Doncaster. 12 May 1963*

Cardiff

During the early spring, I went on several visits to Cardiff (General). Unfortunately my mode of traction from Birmingham (Snow Hill) turned out to be in the form of the brand new cross country multiple units which operated to Swansea. I was never once steam hauled to Cardiff which, considering the many teething troubles suffered by the earlier diesels was a trifle unfortunate. This service to South Wales traversed different routes either via the North Warwickshire line to Gloucester or via Kidderminster and Hereford. To my disappointment neither of these routes went through the Severn Tunnel and even to this day I have still not been through it.

Whilst in transit to Cardiff, I had on one occasion my only look at one of the more famous members of the "Castle" class, No 4073 *Caerphilly Castle*, on a north-west express. I was lucky in this respect, as she must have been on one of her last workings before withdrawal. Another vivid memory of these journeys was the 'copping' of the last steam locomotive built for British Railways '9F' 2-10-0 No 92220 *Evening Star* at Newport on the up "Red Dragon". My favourite stretch of track on these trips was between Newport and Cardiff where the lines were at least quadrupled all the way. After passing the large steam shed at Ebbw Junction there was an endless stream of freights all nose to tail, a trainspotter's paradise. I even copped a narrow gauge V of R loco No 9 *Prince of Wales* on this section. It was on a low loader, making its way back to Aberystwyth after overhaul at Swindon.

These visits to Cardiff proved most rewarding as apart from copping a number of "Halls", "Granges" and countless unnamed engines I was able to polish off most of my remaining "Castles" from Landore. Although I never actually went round Cardiff (Canton), there was a long footbridge at the front of the depot where many engines could be spotted working on and off the shed without incurring the wrath of the staff working there. These

Class 04/8 2-8-0 No 63858. 36A Doncaster. 12 May 1963

trips were most enjoyable except for the one occasion when I made the mistake of going on a Sunday: it was terrible, there were no freights and very few passenger workings.

Rugby

My new regular venue for many Saturdays during the summer service of 1960 (more for a change than anything else) was Rugby (Midland). This was an extremely busy station, being on the West Coast main line, and also a junction for lines to Birmingham, Leicester, Peterborough and Northampton. An added attraction was the crossing of the main line to the south of the station by the ex Great Central over a massive stone viaduct and iron girder bridge, known as the 'birdcage'.

A4 Class 4-6-2 No 60029 Woodcock *at 36A Doncaster. 12 May 1963. Loco was based at Kings Cross, then only one month off closure.*

4F 0-6-0 No 44071 in store at 41E Stavely Barrow Hill. 12 May 1963

B1 4-6-0 No 61090. 41F Mexborough. 12 May 1963

'Royal Scot' Class 4-6-0 No 46141 The North Staffordshire Regiment *outside Rugby Testing Station. 1 June 1963*

Although the station staff at Rugby were not averse to trainspotters, because it was not very easy to obtain the numbers of locos crossing on the GC, many spotters used to make their way by road and trainspot by the girder bridge on an embankment alongside the down main lines. Despite being a convenient location for spotting, it was not however 100 per cent safe as every now and again the police would move us off. I always found it was better to keep on walking until the next road bridge was reached, cross the lines and then gain access to a vacant field. This brought me to a position in the triangle of the main lines and those from Peterborough, with ideal viewing access to the GC and also all of the workings from the shed. This made it well worth the long walk from the station.

Although there were not many named engines to be seen on the GC there was plenty of variety: LMS tanks, and Class 5 4-6-0's, ER V2s, B1s, B16s, 01/04s and L1 tanks, BR Class 5s, WDs and 9Fs. The GC had a fantastic coal train service which must have been the fastest in Britain, hauled in the most part by 9F 2-10-0s from Annesley. Now alas, most of the GC is closed and the proud depots that once stood at Annesley and Woodford Halse are long gone. On odd occasions engines from the WR could be observed and I even copped a "County" No 1015 *County of Gloucester* on a parcels train.

Although during 1960, the EE Type 4s were flooding the main line in ever increasing numbers, steam remained plentiful. In fact it amazed me how long many of the premier steam locos of the LMR continued to be at the head of major express workings. It could be said that their presence on the West Coast main line, south of Crewe, was not taken away in total until 1964. Considering the "Coronations" and their like had reigned supreme for some thirty years, no less than three generations of main line diesels were used in a matter of seven years. If this made economic sense, prior to electrification, then I'm a Dutchman. So much for the experts!

On two consecutive Saturdays in 1960 I copped my last two remaining "Coronations" Nos 46224 *Princess Alexandra* and 46223 *Princess Alice* in that order, both from Polmadie and co-incidentally on the same train, the morning express from Euston to Perth. Another notable named cop was "Britannia" No 70046 *Anzac.*

Rugby shed was adjacent to the London side of the station but because there was a huge glass screen typical of many LNW stations running the entire length of the platform it was all but impossible to see any locos on the depot. The shed was a hard nut to crack as the main entrance was situated at road level with the foreman's office close at hand. A few of the more intrepid spotters would cross the main lines and gain entry that way but it was dangerous and asked for trouble. I got round successfully on two occasions, but so dreaded the prospect of being caught that I gave up the practice.

The reason why I succeeded where others failed was in adopting a new approach to the problem. I used to leave my duffle bag in one of the station lockers and having got rid of this obvious piece of spotter's evidence would then make my way to the official entrance and walk brazenly in, past the office and inside the shed. This approach was to prove overwhelmingly successful over the years, for by acting normally, the majority of shed staff would be under the impression that I had permission to be there and the older and more experienced I got the less likely were the chances of being stopped and ejected. If one was hesitant and unsure inside sheds it often invited (at the very least) curious glances. There were never many rare engines to be seen at Rugby shed but I did see my only B17 4-6-0 No 61660 *Hull City* there shortly before withdrawal.

One Saturday I went from Rugby to Leicester (Midland) to try my luck at spotting some of my remaining "Jubilees" based there and from Kentish Town. Sure enough I was in luck and I saw quite a number of them and also had the pleasure of seeing the "Thames Clyde" express for the first time.

York

By the autumn of 1960, Laira (Plymouth) had lost most of its "Kings" and at long last I was able to cop my two remaining ones, Nos 6026 *King John* and 6029 *King Edward VIII,* both at Snow Hill after transfer to this route. I then decided it was about time I made an effort to see more ex LNER locos and so I made the first of many trips to York. Although the express services from Birmingham had for some time been in the hands of "Peaks" the route through Burton, Derby and Sheffield still had plenty of

4-6-0 No 1014 County of Glamorgan *at Shirley on the 5.45 pm Birmingham (Snow Hill) to Worcester express. 21 June 1963*

steam to offer. The station at York was, and still is, a lovely place with its commanding roof. Despite ever increasing numbers of EE Type 4s being introduced on the East Coast main line, the "Deltics" had not yet arrived and most of the expresses were still steam hauled. For an almost first time spotter the place was a paradise and on this first visit amongst many other "Pacifics", I copped A4 No 60022 *Mallard.*

I was by now getting more experienced and confident in my abilities to get round sheds and much preferred to go round them on my own as there was less risk of being caught. York shed had a huge yard, most of it being accessible from the main road which also provided an easy escape route.

U Class 2-6-0 No 31633 entering Pokesdown Station en route to Bournemouth. 22 June 1963

"Merchant Navy" Class 4-6-2 No 35014 Nederland Line *on the empty stock of the 4.55 pm to Waterloo. Exeter Central. 23 June 1963.*

57XX Class 0-6-0 PT No 9636. 84H Wellington. 16 July 1963

A3 Class No 60084 Trigo. *55H Leeds (Neville Hill) 28 July 1963*

There were over 100 steam locos on shed including my first look at the famous V2 2-6-2 No 60800 *Green Arrow* and I completed my visit without incident. I was to visit this depot many times in the coming years, mostly unofficially, but not once did I get thrown out. Little did I realise on this first visit that in years to come I would be taking my wife and children on a tour of the same roundhouses, in rather different circumstances, after it had become the National Railway Museum.

Railway Enthusiasts Club

As 1960 drew to a close, although I had been on more visits to different venues and had some memorable cops, it occurred to me that if I was to reach the ultimate goal of spotting as many locos as possible, I would have to add to the normal ways of doing it. So I decided to join a loco spotters club based in Birmingham. It was known simply as the Railway Enthusiasts Club and they did many visits to loco sheds either by coach or rail. I did a lot of trips with them and thoroughly enjoyed myself until the club folded in late 1962.

It was organised and run by a committee, most of whom worked on the railway. I did not realise for some time that the organisers very rarely seemed to bother with or go out of their way to obtain shed permits. A classic example to the contrary occurred whilst visiting Hasland shed. This depot was in the middle of nowhere with only a sulphur works for company. It consisted of a solitary roundhouse with walls, but no roof and on a Sunday all the locos on shed were invariably out of steam. It was a long walk to the shed and anticipating no trouble the organiser of our trip decided to remain with the coach. On arrival at the depot we were confronted by the foreman who demanded to see a permit; as none was forthcoming he became rather irate, threw us out and proceeded to follow us back to the coach. After the long walk he stormed up to the organiser, red in the face from his exertions and threatened that he would take the registration number of the coach and report the society, when to everyones utter astonishment the organiser casually reached into his pocket and produced a permit which left the foreman utterly speechless!

In most cases, because of their railway background, the committee used to rely on talking their way round steam sheds.On the odd occasion though, when it became obvious that permission would not be granted, their attitude would become one of — "Be as quick as you can lads" — "Disperse widely once in the shed so as to confuse the foreman/shedmaster but we will stay on the coach".

I used to hero worship one or two members of the committee because they only needed a handful of steam locos from around the country, as was the case of the club organiser, whom I will refer to henceforth as "The Leader". My first trip with the society was at the end of 1960, by train to the Chester and Birkenhead areas, not the most glamorous of sheds but it was a good start towards becoming a real trainspotter.

'Royal Scot' Class 4-6-0 No 46165 The Ranger (12th London Regt.) *at 5A Crewe (North). 29 September 1963.*

'Coronation' Class 4-6-2 No 46228 Duchess of Rutland *at 5A Crewe (North). 29 September 1963.*

Kings Unthroned
1961-1962

1961 began with rail visits by the REC to sheds in the Derby, Nottingham and Lincoln areas but my first recorded trip with them (in early April) was again by rail to sheds in Manchester. Over 400 steam locos were seen including the now preserved "Director" No 62660 *Butler Henderson* which was then in Gorton Works for restoration. This was followed in early May by a coach trip to sheds in the Leeds area, of which unfortunately, I have no records. It was after this trip that I decided to keep permanent comprehensive records of all major trips.

The sheds at Worcester, Gloucester, Swindon, Didcot and Oxford were visited by coach in late May and some 175 steam locos were seen at Swindon shed and works alone, including eighteen "Castles" and five "Kings". The first of the new "Western" diesel hydraulics, which all too soon were to sound the death knell for the "Kings" were in the process of being constructed. I remember a discussion between two spotters as to whether or not they could smuggle a nameplate out of the works and the ludicrous suggestion was to use duffle bags to cover the ends of the plate and then use a human screen round the rest of it. The idea never came to fruition because as they tried to lift it they found it was much heavier than they expected!

I left school in June 1961 and although I had expressed a desire to go to Tyseley shed to work I was talked out of it. It was to be another three years before I eventually got a job on the railway.

The next major trip by coach with the REC was to the Central, West and South regions of Wales, where over 700 steam locos were seen. Many of the sheds visited were in delightful backwaters like Cardigan, Milford Haven, Upper Bank, Neath N & B, Burry Port, and Lydney, and during the course of this trip I copped the majority of my remaining named ex-GWR locos.

The following tour in August was a golden one for cops, my first venture in Southern territory. We travelled to London first of all on the 1.00 a.m. train from Snow Hill, where at Paddington we would transfer to a coach for the shed visits. It was a strange train with no particular return working travelling via the tedious route of Oxford and Didcot, its importance being a newspaper train, with a few carriages for passengers. From memory, it arrived at Paddington around 5.00 a.m.

The coach took us to the majority of sheds on the Central and Eastern divisions of the Southern where in excess of 450 steam locos were seen, all but a handful being cops for me. As a measure of how rapidly things were to change, out of fourteen steam sheds visited on this day, I was to revisit only four of them at later dates still with steam allocations.

In September, I again went to York by train for the day and although the "Deltics" were being introduced the position had not changed a lot from 1960. A very proud cop for me was 4-6-2 No 70000 *Britannia*, much sought after by spotters from Birmingham. It must have been a rarity in its own right, even at York. Several spotters gathered round the loco and were allowed to 'cab' her until the train crew realised that many of them were helping themselves to lumps of coal as mementoes.

The last months of 1961 saw visits to sheds in the Derby, Nottingham, Leicester and East Anglian areas, which altogether produced some 1000 steam engines. I copped another famous engine during one of these visits A3 No 60103 *Flying Scotsman* at New England shed and it was interesting to see the experimental gas-turbine 4-6-0 GT3 at Leicester GC. So ended my first year with a Society and not counting the unrecorded steam locos, over 2500 were noted. This was indeed the real way to trainspot!

1962

After the experiences of 1961 I was determined to go on as many Society trips as my pocket could afford. To give some idea of how cheap most of these trips were I have reproduced the proposed itinerary of club trips during 1962 and the costs.

Rebuilt 'Patriot' Class No 45530 Sir Frank Ree *ex Works at 5B Crewe (South). 29 September 1963. One of the last surviving LMS named locomotives.*

Shed Visits proposed by the Railway Enthusiasts Club

January 1962-July 1962

NOTE — STP — Subject to permit

Sunday 7 Jan 40E Colwick, 41E Staveley (Barrow Hill), 41H Staveley G.C., 41B Grimesthorpe, 41A Sheffield (Darnall), 41D Canklow, 41F Mexborough, 36A Doncaster, 36C Frodingham, 40B Immingham & Doncaster Works — fare 18/-.

Sunday 21 Jan 72A Exmouth Jct., Seaton, Lyme Regis, Bridport, 72C Yeovil, 82G Templecombe, 71G Weymouth, Branksome, 71B Bournemouth, Lymington, 71I Southampton Docks, 71A Eastleigh, Eastleigh Works, Winchester, 70C Guildford, 81D Reading & Reading South —fare 37/6.

Sunday 11 Feb 55A Leeds (Holbeck)—STP, 55D Royston, 55C Farnley Jct., 55B Stourton, 55E Normanton, 55F Manningham, 55G Huddersfield, 55H Leeds (Neville Hill), 56A Wakefield, 56B Ardsley, 56C Copley Hill, 56D Mirfield & 56F Low Moor — fare 17/-.

Sunday 4 March 84A Wolverhampton (Stafford Road), 84B Oxley, 84H Wellington, 21C Bushbury, 89A Shrewsbury & Wolverhampton Works — fare 12/-.

Saturday & Sunday 24/25 March 50D Goole, 50A York, 51J Northallerton, 51F West Auckland, 52K Consett, 52C Blaydon, 52F North & South Blyth, 52E Percy Main, 52A Gateshead, 52B Heaton, Bowes Bridge, Pelton Level, 52H Tyne Dock, 52G Sunderland, 51L Thornaby, 51C West Hartlepool, 51A Darlington, Darlington Works & scrapyard, and 50E Scarborough. Price including B & B 55/-.

Sunday 8 April 17B Burton, 17A Derby, Derby Works, 5F Uttoxeter, 5D Stoke, 5E Alsager, Crewe Works, 5A Crewe (North), 5B Crewe (South), Whitchurch, 89D Oswestry, Oswestry Works, 89A Shrewsbury & 84H Wellington — fare 17/-.

Saturday & Sunday 28/29 April 72E Barnstaple, Torrington, Launceston, Okehampton, 72F Wadebridge, St. Ives, 83G Penzance, Helston, 83F Truro, 83E St. Blazey, Moorswater, 83H Plymouth (Friary), 83D Laira (Plymouth), 83A Newton Abbot, 83C Exeter, 72A Exmouth Jct., Tiverton & 83B Taunton — fare 45/-.

Sunday 20 May 81A Old Oak Common, 1A Willesden, 14D Neasden, 14A Cricklewood, 14B Kentish Town, 1B Camden, 34A Kings Cross, 34B Hornsey, 34G Finsbury Park, 30A Stratford, 33A Plaistow, 1D Devons Road, 70A Nine Elms, 70B Feltham, 73A Stewarts Lane (STP), & 81C Southall — fare 22/6.

Sunday 17 June 85A Worcester, 85B Gloucester Horton Road, 85C Gloucester Barnwood, Swindon Works, 82C Swindon, Chippenham, 82F Bath Green Park, Radstock, Frome, 82D Westbury, 72B Salisbury, Andover, 81D Reading, 81E Didcot & 84C Banbury — fare 19/-.

Saturday & Sunday 14/15 July 24J Lancaster (Green Ayre), 12G Oxenholme, 12H Tebay, 12D Kirkby Stephen, Penrith, 12C Carlisle (Canal), 12A Carlisle (Kingmoor), 12B Carlisle (Upperby), 12F Workington, 12E Barrow, 24L Carnforth, 24H Hellifield, 24G Skipton, Keighley, 56E Sowerby Bridge & 9D Buxton — fare 37/6.

My first trip in 1962 with the REC was in January to sheds in the South West and South Coast of England. The weather was atrocious, it poured with rain for the entire duration and got heavier as the day progressed. For those who remember spotting in such conditions, they were a nightmare for writing down numbers of engines without the book getting soaked. For those who had only biros it was almost impossible, and the only effective way of getting over this problem was to crouch by the motions of locomotives which offered at least scant protection. At Weymouth we faced a very long walk to the shed, the rain was coming down in sheets and we got drenched. I remember spending the remainder of the coach journey wrapped in newspaper in a vain attempt to blot up some of the water in my clothes. Still it was all good fun. I copped eleven "Lord Nelsons", forty eight "West Countries/Battle of Britains" and ten "Merchant Navy" locos, apart from many others.

A trip to Leeds in February was followed by a mammoth one to the North East over two days, with an overnight stay in Whitley Bay. Nineteen sheds were visited which produced the massive total of 796 steam and 174 diesels, not bad for a weekend and all for the princely sum of 55s 0d (£2.75 pence). Of the sheds visited, Thornaby had the most with 117 steam locos alone.

The highlight of this particular trip was the visit to Gateshead. After we arrived at our digs for the overnight stay, our leader informed us that he had no permit for this shed. From previous experience he advised us not to go, as it would be dark and Gateshead was extremely hard to bunk and also dangerous. In those days a third rail system operated around Newcastle and the shed was situated with the River Tyne on one side, surrounded by electrified tracks. Nevertheless, the lure of LNER "Pacifics" was too much for the majority. We caught a train to Newcastle and walked to the depot across the High Level bridge, it was an eerie place which I remember was gas-lit and infested with Teddy Boys.

After a preliminary scout round for unofficial entrances we could find one only, on the north side of the shed up a set of shaky wooden stairs. After skirting alongside a carriage shed we realised what our leader had said about it being a hard nut to crack. The shed yard was a large open area illuminated by floodlights, where anything bigger than a rabbit could be spotted from the shedmaster's office. To attempt a mass run by some thirty or so spotters across the yard to the roundhouses would have meant being trapped and consequently easy prey for the shed staff and police.

We were about to give up and return to the station when fortune smiled in the shape of A3 4-6-2 No 60039 *Sandwich.* This loco had either been taking on water or coal only a few yards from us when she slowly started to make her way across the yard. In an instant all of us were walking alongside the loco, out of sight of those in the office, until we reached the comparative safety of the darker section of the yard. At the far side of the depot was a small straight shed and an open roundhouse. One of our number succeeded in falling into a pit, fortunately without injury. Once round the shed, exit out of the way we had come in was quite easy.

On the train back to our digs we congratulated ourselves on what must rank as one of the most spectacular bunking deeds in the annals of trainspotting. We had achieved total success on our mission and had spotted forty-four steam engines we would not otherwise have seen including five A4 4-6-2s Nos 60001 *Sir Ronald Matthews,* 60002 *Sir Murrough Wilson,* 60005 *Sir Charles Newton,* 60007 *Sir Nigel Gresley,* 60018 *Sparrow Hawk* and six A3 4-6-2s Nos 60039 *Sandwich,* 60042 *Singapore,* 60045 *Lemberg,* 60052 *Prince Palatine,* 60078 *Night Hawk* and 60084 *Trigo.* When we got back to our digs, the ones who had chickened out of the venture were consumed with envy as we gloated over our triumph and waved our notebooks under their noses. The landlady must have thought we were all off our trollies. I have often wondered what the coach drivers thought of our antics, a change from taking old ladies to the seaside!

'-6-0 No 7804 Baydon Manor *at 87F Llanelly 22 March 1964. The author's last major steam trip round South Wales sheds. Only a handful of these steam sheds were still active in 1965*

Class 3 2-6-2T No 82019 ex Works at 70D Eastleigh. 24 May 1964

Class 4 2-6-0 No 76114 on station pilot duties at Glasgow (St Enoch). 1 August 1964

Many of the depots in the North East were in desolate surroundings and in run down condition. None more so than places like Consett and Tyne Dock. How on earth they got people to work there I will never know. Apart from modern classes like the B1 4-6-0s and 9F 2-10-0s, the North East seemed to be inundated with ancient machines and yet some classes like the Q6 0-8-0s and J27 0-6-0s were to survive in part for another five and a half years.

The next trip with the REC was an overnight one to Devon and Cornwall at the end of April. After doing Barnstaple, an attempt to find Launceston shed in the dark ended in complete farce. Although someone on the coach thought they had found the relevant railway line, the driver got himself lost and refused to continue driving up narrow country lanes. In a last desperate attempt to find the shed, we all got out of the coach and after dispersing in different directions over various fields and peering over hedges, we gave up.

The diesels in Devon and Cornwall were by now really starting to bite. After visiting Penzance, Helston, Truro, St. Blazey and Moorswater we had seen only twenty-seven steam locos, but things picked up at Plymouth when we saw a further forty-six at Laira and some others at Friary. At Newton Abbot I copped my last "Castle" No 5003 *Lulworth Castle* which was in the company of four others Nos 4098 *Kidwelly Castle,* 5024 *Carew Castle,* 5055 *Earl of Eldon* and 5098 *Clifford Castle.* We had a guide round this shed and he specifically requested that we steered clear of a freshly concreted area. As usual there is always one fellow who is oblivious to most things and sure enough a few minutes later we heard a 'splish-splash' noise, only to find that this fellow had walked through the middle of it. The guide's comments were not complimentary!

The final depot of the day was at Taunton and as our leader had no permit access was to be gained by the station platform. Although most railwaymen were of a reasonable nature we were stopped at the end of the platform by a small man, whom by his own admission was a clerk in the offices. He was what I can only describe as a PPO (petty public official). Although entry to the shed did not mean crossing any running lines he made a determined effort to stop us by spreading his arms out to their full extent. We chose to ignore him completely and in his vain attempt he became like "King Canute", engulfed in a sea of spotters. We must have hurt his ego, for we never saw him again.

My next trip with the REC was to London on 20 May. After visiting Willesden, Hornsey, Finsbury Park and Devons Road, we arrived at Kings Cross; my only visit to the Top Shed where thirty-six steam locos were on view including nine A4s Nos 60003 *Andrew K. McCosh,* 60006 *Sir Ralph Wedgwood,* 60010 *Dominion of Canada,* 60021 *Wild Swan,* 60022 *Mallard,* 60026 *Miles Beevor,* 60029 *Woodcock,* 60032 *Gannet* and 60033 *Seagull.*

Next on the list came Stratford. In its heyday it had the largest steam allocation in the land, but was sadly depleted with only fifty-four seen on our visit. Our guide was a compulsive talker — until an incident happened! On approaching the workshops he informed us that it was out of bounds, giving no reason why. However a main door was open wide revealing several steam locos. What happened next was spontaneous; a number of spotters slipped through the door and were soon followed by the remainder, leaving the guide to carry on walking and talking, oblivious of the fact he was now on his own. We swarmed round the works like ants frantically writing numbers down before he returned. He appeared at the door red in the face and blowing a whistle. After reluctantly accepting our excuse that we had not heard his instructions we carried on, but he hardly spoke again, which was a welcome relief.

Further sheds on the itinerary were Plaistow, Kentish Town, Cricklewood, Nine Elms, Feltham and Stewarts Lane. This latter depot was a shadow of its former self with only eight steam engines to be seen including Nos 30926 *Repton,* 34089 *602 Squadron,* 34100 *Appledore* and 34101 *Hartland.* The fifteen sheds visited produced around 400 steam.

My last trip with the REC was to the Carlisle and Cumbria areas in late July. After doing Tebay shed in the dead of night, "Jubilee" No 45726 *Vindictive* roared down Shap and passed us on an overnight express, a wonderful sight. This was my first shed bash in this area, giving an opportunity to spot many of my remaining "Jubilees" from Carlisle. Kingmoor was a steam Mecca with ninety locos on shed, "Princess" No 46203 *Princess Margaret Rose* was in steam and amongst the total were six "Coronations" Nos 46226 *Duchess of Norfolk,* 46227 *Duchess of Devonshire,* 46231 *Duchess of Atholl,* 46244 *King George VI,* 46247 *City of Liverpool,* and 46257 *City of Salford.* As we departed, "Scot" No 46129 *The Scottish Horse*

Class J38 0-6-0 No 65901 at 65A Eastfield (Glasgow). 1 August 1964. Eastfield was a collecting point for locos going to Cowlairs and St Rollox Works

'Jubilee' Class No 45597 Barbados *at 50B Hull (Dairycoats). 10 April 1965*

Rebuilt 'Battle of Britain' 4-6-2 No 34082 615 Squadron *at 70F Bournemouth. 23 May 1965*

Class 04/4 2-8-0 No 63868 on the coal stage at 41H Staveley G.C. on 10 June 1965. The depot was closed a few days later

stormed toward Glasgow, deputising for a diesel on a late overnight express from Birmingham.

After Kingmoor, Canal shed was an anticlimax with only twenty-five steam but Upperby produced a further sixty-six to make the total for the three Carlisle sheds 181.

Workington and Barrow sheds were visited after Carlisle, the latter shed being one of the last bastions for the MR 2F 0-6-0s of which Nos 58120/60/77/82 were present. On then to Carnforth, where one of the last unrebuilt "Patriots" was in steam No 45543 *Home Guard*. We progressed across country to Hellifield, which had an air of desolation with just one loco in steam out of seventeen. A rarity was Corkerhill "Jubilee" No 45673 *Keppel*. Our final sheds of the day were Skipton, Sowerby Bridge, Keighley and Heaton Mersey. Yet again in excess of 400 steam were seen in one day.

For some time a friend and myself had been planning a week's holiday in Scotland, using a railrover ticket in an effort to visit as many sheds as was possible. We arranged to stay on alternate nights with my aunt in Aviemore. We worked out an itinerary with a Scottish Region timetable and I sent off for permits for the sheds we hoped to visit. I was pleasantly surprised to get them in a short space of time, but for some strange reason they were in the name of P. B. McIndoe. It was a comforting thought to have these passes instead of having to try and bunk every shed.

We left Birmingham on the 18 August and made our way to Aviemore where we stayed until the 20th. Despite dieselisation of the routes north of Perth and most of the West Highland line, Scotland still had plenty of steam to offer. On the 20th, our first port of call, shed-wise was Ayr, where thirty-nine steam were on shed including many Caledonian locos, most sadly stored in various stages of dereliction, though some were active on freights in the area. We progressed to Kilmarnock where within a short space of time we observed three steam hauled expresses, "Coronation" No 46227 *Duchess of Devonshire,* Glasgow-Carlisle; "Britannia" No 70051 *Firth of Forth,* Carlisle-Glasgow; and the up "Thames-Clyde" doubleheaded by A3 No 60038 *Firdaussi* and "Britannia" No 70052 *Firth of Tay.* We had to be content with a mere BR 2-6-4 T on a local for Darvel, the station for Hurlford, where fifty-six locos were seen of various types. From Kilmarnock we progressed to Carlisle, passing Dumfries shed yard which had many Caledonian locos in steam.

21 August—We made an attempt to bunk Kingmoor in the dark, but whilst in the shed yard were warned by a driver that police were present and so we gave up, but I was lucky enough to cop my last "Scot" No 46133 *The Green Howards.* We spent a rather cold and sleepless night on Citadel Station before catching an early morning express to Glasgow. As we were travelling to a terminal station it enabled us to catch up on some sleep, a welcome contrast to the hard work of keeping awake whilst dog tired and having to detrain at an intermediate station. After arrival at Central Station we spent most of the day travelling by bus to the Glasgow sheds. Our first stop was Dawsholm, a rather nondescript shed with a meagre allocation and we were rather surprised to be confronted by an immaculate inspector who demanded to see our shed pass. Only fifteen locos were on shed including the preserved locos *Gordon Highlander, Glen Douglas* and the "Jones Goods" along with the ill fated 4-4-0 No 54398 *Ben Alder.*

On then to Eastfield which, despite increasing dieselisation, still had a large steam allocation of which forty-eight examples were present. From here we went to St. Rollox, the shed for Buchanan Street. The depot was rather run down and had seen better days, but thirty-seven locos were here; three of them "Pacifics" Nos 60011 *Empire of India,* 60027 *Merlin* and 60162 *Saint Johnstoun.* We made our way to Cowlairs Works for the appointed time on the permit and after a short wait the guide read out a list

Line up of locos at 41H Staveley 10 June 1965 (1-to-r.) WD 2-8-0 No 90227; 04/8 2-8-0 No 63701; 04/4 No 63863

of names, all of which were duly answered until he got to a Mr. McIndoe. He repeated the name several times before I realised it was the name on my permit and rather sheepishly I said I was present. The works was sparsely populated with only nineteen engines including a "Clan" No 72009 *Clan Stewart*.

On then to Polmadie; what a magnificent shed it must have been in its heyday, bearing in mind it was a weekday, over seventy steam locos were seen including seven "Coronations" Nos 46222 *Queen Mary*, 46223 *Princess Alice*, 46224 *Princess Alexandra*, 46230 *Duchess of Buccleuch*, 46231 *Duchess of Atholl*, 46232 *Duchess of Montrose* and 46242 *City of Glasgow*, though none were in steam. Also ten Caledonians were present, including two of the last 4-4-0s Nos 54463 and 54502, both stored.

Our last shed of the day was Corkerhill where we found forty-three steam. Dead in the yard were five "Jubilees", the others of the class allocated to this depot being in store at Lugton. For some reason the Scottish Region seemed to dislike these locos, as they were all withdrawn by the end of 1962. From here we returned to the city centre and to Aviemore for a welcome night's rest.

22 August — We travelled to Aberdeen via Inverness and headed for Ferryhill. Somehow we ended up in an allotment on the walk to the shed, the owner not being too impressed as he thought we were after his prize vegetables. The depot had a distinct air of grandeur about it with five "Pacifics" amongst the total of twenty-nine steam — Nos 60004 *William Whitelaw*, 60009 *Union of South Africa*, 60159 *Bonnie Dundee*, 60161 *North British* and 60534 *Irish Elegance*. On our return to the station, A2 No 60525 *A H Peppercorn* was at the head of an express to Glasgow but we were disappointed to find a diesel on our train to Dundee.

The journey there was uneventful but the carriage sidings north of the station held a filthy A3 No 60087 *Blenheim* on empty stock. In contrast, Tay Bridge shed had four immaculate A2s Nos 60519 *Honeyway,* 60528 *Tudor Minstrel,* 60532 *Blue Peter* and 60536 *Trimbush* in company with thirty-one other steam locos. Thornton Junction and Dunfermline had seventy-five steam between them. As the evening approached we made our way to Perth and were fortunate to spend a comfortable night in an empty stock train in a bay platform.

23 August — Our next venues were the Edinburgh sheds and we set off from Perth early in the morning behind a Carlisle "Jubilee" No 45741 *Leinster.* Our train went via Dunfermline and we were banked up to the Forth Bridge by an elderly 0-6-0 No 64480. At Queensferry we were passed by A4 No 60012 *Commonwealth of Australia* on a three coach local!

Despite large numbers of main line diesels, Haymarket shed still housed a number of "Pacifics". I remember a colour photo of an A4 proudly displayed in the shedmaster's office which I think was No 60024 *Kingfisher,* but unfortunately A4s were not present on this occasion. There were however, five A3s Nos 60097 *Humorist,* 60098 *Spion Kop,* 60099 *Call Boy,* 60100 *Spearmint* and 60101 *Cicero* on shed. We then went to Dalry Road, a depot situated in rather drab surroundings, which contained twenty-nine steam, with D49 4-4-0 No 62712 *Morayshire* awaiting preservation. From here we progressed to St Margarets, a very busy shed with a large allocation of which seventy-two were present, mostly freight types with only A3 No 60089 *Felstead* of note.

Class 5 4-6-0 No 45118 at 12B Carlisle (Upperby) 11·6·65.

A begrimed 'Britania' Class No 70026 Polar Star *shorn of nameplates at Lancaster (Green Ayre). 11 June 1965*

4-6-0 No 6831 Bearley Grange *passes through Leamington with a heavily loaded South Coast holiday express. 26 June 1965*

From Edinburgh we went by bus to Bathgate which was to become infamous over the years as a large dump for condemned steam. Thirty-five locos were on shed; seventeen stored, consisting mainly of the older types of classes including two 4-4-0s Nos 62484 *Glen Lyon* and 62685 *Malcolm Graeme.* We left this shed, and through a variety of ways, headed back to Aviemore.

24 August — After bidding farewell to my aunt we looked forward to the remaining two days of our holiday and travelled back to Edinburgh again. On passing Haymarket I copped a Gateshead A3 No 60060 *The Tetrarch.* We visited St. Margarets again to find that many of the locos were different to our visit the previous day, including three more "Pacifics" Nos 60041 *Salmon Trout,* 60043 *Brown Jack* and 60530 *Sayajirao.* Leaving Edinburgh, we stopped at Polmont shed where we found the twenty-one occupants all in store. From Polmont we journeyed via Glasgow to Motherwell, a busy freight shed surrounded by grim factories belching out clouds of sulphurous fumes. There were sixty-three locos on shed, including twenty-two Caledonians and eight WD 2-10-0s. These latter engines were very powerful and most were in Scotland allocated to Motherwell and Grangemouth. From Motherwell we moved south to Carlisle for our last night.

The last 'Castle' in service. No 7029 Clun Castle *in steam at 85B Gloucester (Horton Road). 1 August 1965. Preserved at Birmingham Railway Museum, Tyseley*

Line up of redundant pannier tanks at 88B Cardiff Radyr on 1 August 1965. The shed had closed to steam a few days earlier. No 9622 is the main loco

25 August — We decided Kingmoor was too dangerous to bunk and went to Upperby instead, where we found fifty-five steam before returning to the station. It was a very interesting night as many of the Anglo-Scottish expresses were in the hands of steam some of the notable ones being Nos 46137 *The Prince of Wales's Volunteers* (South Lancashire) and 72006 *Clan Mackenzie* on the down "Northern Irishman", No 46135 *The East Lancashire Regiment,* Glasgow-Euston, No 45528 *R.E.M.E.*, on the down "Royal Highlander", No 46235 *City of Birmingham,* Glasgow-Birmingham, No 46249 *City of Sheffield,* Euston-Perth and No 46252 *City of Leicester,* Glasgow-Euston. After leaving Carlisle we headed towards Birmingham,changed trains at Crewe and were hauled home on the final leg by "Scot" No 46116 *Irish Guardsman.* We arrived at New Street tired but happy, as we had seen over 1200 steam locos on this mammoth trip.

As the end of the summer service approached, a long taken-for-granted every day occurrence was about to disappear, the end of the "Kings" on the Paddington-Birkenhead expresses. No 6002 *King William IV* spent several days at Snow Hill, on show to the public, and on the very last Saturday a friend and myself spent the day travelling between this station and Leamington in an effort to travel behind as many "Kings" as possible. We were unfortunate in that we had only a run behind one, No 6007 *King William III,* all the rest being "Castles". This particular weekend was not only significant with the surrender of these expresses to diesel power, but it marked the beginning of the wholesale slaughter of steam passenger power on all regions and September 1962 was probably the worst-ever month for withdrawals. With the demise of the "Kings" (although most London expresses were in the hands of diesels) steam was still plentiful at Snow Hill mostly on freights, but the station was never to be quite the same.

After the folding up of the REC and due also to lack of money, I was forced for several months to confine most of my activities to local stations and short distance trips. In late September I made my last visit to Wolverhampton (Stafford Road) where the lines of condemned "Kings" presented a sad sight. Somehow, the depot remained open for another year, by which time the dwindling steam allocation which still included a number of "Castles" was tranferred to Oxley. The railways around Wolverhampton must have employed a huge total of people in steam days, but out of three sheds, Bushbury, Oxley, Stafford Road and Wolverhampton Works all that remains today are the sidings on the site of Oxley.

Early in October I went to Rugby for the day, my first visit since April. On shed were twenty-one steam locos with a further forty observed on the main line and thirty-three crossing on the GC. Being winter service, most of the expresses on the main line were in diesel hands, but steam locos noted of interest were Nos 45668 *Madden,* 45669 *Fisher,* 45670 *Howard of Effingham,* 46119 *Lancashire Fusilier,* 46149 *The Middlesex Regiment,* 70018 *Flying Dutchman* and 70032 *Tennyson;* not a single "Coronation" among them!

'Modified Hall' 4-6-0 No 6999 Capel Dewi Hall *approaches Earlswood signal box with a Kingswear-Wolverhampton express. 7 August 1965*

A1 Class 4-6-2 No 60118 Archibald Sturrock *in steam at 55H Leeds (Neville Hill) 8 August 1965. In background are preserved locos No 61994* The Great Marquess *and No 69621*

In early December I went on my first major shed bashing trip for several months, travelling by rail to Liverpool with the same friend I had been with to Scotland. Being a Sunday, the route was via Rugeley due to engineering works. Two "Black 5s" Nos 45403/95 hauled us as far as Rugeley, where 45495 continued on its own to Crewe, after which an electric loco took over. After arrival at Lime Street we crossed the River Mersey by ferry and went first to Birkenhead where forty-six locos were on shed. Bidston shed was a trainspotter's dream — just six engines and, not surprisingly, soon closed. Walton-on-the-Hill and Aintree produced fifty-one steam and it was not until we reached Edge Hill that we saw any named engines. Sixty-eight locos were on shed, those ones of note being Nos 45526 *Morecambe and Heysham,* 45531 *Sir Frederick Harrison,* 45577 *Bengal,* 45695 *Minotaur,* 46110 *Grenadier Guardsman,* 46114 *Coldstream Guardsman,* 46119 *Lancashire Fusilier,* 46220 *Coronation,* 46229 *Duchess of Hamilton,* 46233 *Duchess of Sutherland,* 46241 *City of Edinburgh,* 46243 *City of Lancaster* and 46257 *City of Salford.*

The final shed of the day was Speke Junction which housed thirty-one steam. Speke stays in my mind as having possibly the worst-ever surroundings to a depot. Drab high rise flats, many of which were vandalised, a procession of litter strewn cul-de-sacs, and the entrance to the shed was through a small tunnel underneath some main lines which was littered with broken prams, bicycles and bottles.

So ended 1962, a disastrous one for BR steam with over 3000 withdrawals. Thanks to increased shed visits, my total of steam seen for the year came to 5011, though many were seen more than once.

Class 5 4-6-0 No 44851 ex Works in the yard at 55B Stourton 8·8·65.

In heavy shadow of nearby cooling towers B1 4-6-0 No 61173 Class 4 2-6-4T No 42269 at 56A Wakefield 8 August 1965

'Jubilee" Class 4-6-0 No 45694 Bellerophon *in company with B1 4-6-0 No 61387 and unidentified WD 2-8-0 at 56A Wakefield. 8 August 1965*

Beginning of the End

1963-1964

The first months of the year were particularly abysmal, with snow, ice and severe temperatures, conditions which kept all but the hardiest of spotters at home, including myself. Apart from the odd visit to local stations and trips to Grantham and Newcastle my steam activities were virtually nil until early May, although I did partake in a farewell run behind the last "King" No 6018 *King Henry VI* from Birmingham to Swindon on 28 April, this being a very sad occasion.

The 12th May saw a steam special to Doncaster from Birmingham(New Street) behind SR "Pacific" No 34094 *Mortehoe.* Derby shed and works were visited before progressing to Doncaster where the shed was choc-a-block with steam,103 of them, twelve being "Pacifics" Nos 60016 *Silver King,* 60029 *Woodcock,* 60077 *The White Knight,* 60119 *Patrick Stirling,* 60125 *Scottish Union,* 60128 *Bongrace,* 60149 *Amadis,* 60156 *Great Central,* 60158 *Aberdonian,* 60520 *Owen Tudor* and 60538 *Velocity.*

Repairs to steam at Doncaster Works were only six months off ceasing, but despite this twenty locos were in for overhaul or ex-works, these included Nos 60006 *Sir Ralph Wedgwood,* 60031 *Golden Plover,* 60054 *Prince of Wales,* 60063 *Isinglass,* 60117 *Bois Roussel,* 60121 *Silurian* and 60152 *Holyrood.* Nos 60022 *Mallard,* 60800 *Green Arrow* and 65567 were in for preservation. A number of "Pacifics" lay around condemned and awaiting the cutter's torch, Nos 60013 *Dominion of New Zealand,* 60014 *Silver Link,* 60015 *Quicksilver,* 60056 *Centenary,* 60078 *Night Hawk,* 60144 *King's Courier,* 60500 *Edward Thompson,* 60521 *Watling Street,* 60525 *A. H. Peppercorn,* 60526 *Sugar Palm* and 60539 *Bronzino.* Although condemned, *Edward Thompson* had had its front bufferbeam repainted, which seemed rather strange and also a waste of money.

At Doncaster Station a Leeds-Kings Cross express arrived behind A3 No 60107 *Royal Lancer.* The loco was immediately besieged by scores of enthusiasts off our special train, and if the train crew were surprised they certainly didn't show it and carried on as if this phenomena was a regular Sunday occurrence.

In early June I visited Rugby for virtually the last time and although steam workings on the main lines had steadily declined, many regular expresses and holiday trains were in steam hands. The day produced no less than five "Coronations", Nos 46228 *Duchess of Rutland,* 46233 *Duchess of Sutherland,* 46245 *City of London,* 46251 *City of Nottingham* and 46256 *Sir William A Stanier F.R.S.*

In the middle of the month I had a week's holiday at Bournemouth and, apart from the station and shed here, I spent many a happy hour at Pokesdown Station to the east of Bournemouth. With a quadrupled track

B1 4-6-0 No 61051 off Langwith Junction in the yard at 55A Leeds (Holbeck) with a Class 5 4-6-0 and an 8F 2-8-0. 8 August 1965

'Modified Hall' 4-6-0 No 7922 Salford Hall *heads a Westbound freight through Earlswood. 8 October 1965*

as far as the latter station, the succession of steam hauled expresses was endless. Bullied "Pacifics" of both the unrebuilt and rebuilt variety roared through the station at high speeds; it was a paradise for steam lovers.

In early July I purchased a 49cc moped and with a top speed of 25 mph it really opened the way towards independent spotting. As I had another week's holiday in the middle of the month I planned a round trip of Wales and somehow managed to attach a huge suitcase and tent to the back of this little bike and off I went. Craven Arms, Shrewsbury, Croes Newyd and Mold sheds were visited before I camped by the North Wales main line at Abergele. It had been a perfect start with beautiful weather and many miles covered.

The following day, a Sunday, I headed for Holyhead. Unfortunately the weather changed and became windy, wet and cold. After visiting Llandudno and Bangor sheds the moped started to play up and kept cutting out every few miles. A Sunday in North Wales in those days was not the place to be when having mechanical troubles and as I was unable to find an open garage I decided to abandon the plan of proceeding to Holyhead and instead headed for the Welsh coast and Barmouth as it was at least a little nearer to home.

In Caernarvon I took the wrong turning and headed off into the mountains. By this time the rain was coming down in sheets, driven by gale force winds. For a while I was able to beg shelter in a roadmender's hut with some workmen who made it more than obvious that they resented my presence. I decided to brave the weather rather than put up with their mutterings and glarings and headed deeper into the hills on my spluttering bike. The weather deteriorated so much I was forced to stop and in vain I tried to pitch my tent. It proved impossible and I began to wish that I had taken an uncle's advice of many years previous, when he had suggested I took up stamp collecting! In the end I was able to spend the night in a farmer's barn, which was a welcome relief.

The following day the weather was similar, but nevertheless I pressed on. However, with these conditions and continual breakdowns I had had enough by the time I reached Barmouth. I had bed and breakfast and the next day set off for home. The gods were still against me as I even got kicked out of Machynlleth shed, which contained only half a dozen engines. I eventually arrived home and consulted the moped's handbook (which I hadn't bothered to read before setting out) and found that I should have used more oil with the petrol whilst the bike was still new.

Some of my friends also purchased mopeds and we often went round the Birmingham sheds on them on Sundays. One of these depots was Aston, a particularly hard depot to bunk, as at first we could find only one entrance — the official one. This led us past the shedmaster's office and invariably we were nobbled and ejected. Barry, or as he preferred to be called, Baz, found an alternative entrance on one visit. As we were descending the steps to the shed, he leaned over the wall to discover a pile of coke a few feet below him and from now on we used this thoughtful amenity to gain entrance. This method continued until one day Baz leapt over the wall without looking to find to his horror that the coke had gone! Despite the long drop Baz did not hurt himself, but I will never forget the look on his face. Disaster was to occur many times to the unfortunate Baz before steam finished.

In late September I travelled behind "Coronation" No 46245 *City of London* on a special to Crewe, from Snow Hill, organised by the Warwickshire Railway Society. We visited both depots and the works. Crewe (South) contained eighty-seven steam, mostly freight locos, but the north shed was a real eye-opener. Despite many years of increasing modernisation, there were no less than thirty named passenger locos to be seen, most of which were still in service — Nos 45534 *E. Tootal Broadhurst,* 45552 *Silver Jubilee,* 45554 *Ontario,* 45556 *Novia Scotia,* 45567 *South Australia,* 45586 *Mysore,* 45591 *Udaipur,* 45595 *Southern Rhodesia,* 45666 *Cornwallis,* 45689 *Ajax,* 45704 *Leviathan,* 45717 *Dauntless,* 45721 *Impregnable,* 45726 *Vindictive,* 46144 *Honourable Artillery Company,* 46155 *The Lancer,* 46165 *The Ranger (12th London Regt.),* 46228 *Duchess of Rutland,* 46245 *City of London,* 46248 *City of Leeds,* 46251 *City of Nottingham,* 46256 *Sir William A. Stanier F.R.S.,* 70017 *Arrow,* 70019 *Lightning,* 70023 *Venus,* 70027 *Rising Star,* 70042 *Lord Roberts,* 70050 *Firth of Clyde,* 70052 *Firth of Tay* and 70054 *Dornoch Firth.* It was a magnificent array and one could be forgiven for thinking that it was the 1950s over again, but in reality it was a swan-song gathering as for many of these locos the deepening gloom was approaching rapidly. The ill-starred No 71000 *Duke of Gloucester* was stored inside the shed and it was to be a very different Crewe (North) I was to visit again in 1965.

BR Class 9F 2-10-0 No 92227 passing Earlswood. This was one of the last steam locos seen on the North Warwickshire line, all freights were withdrawn shortly after this photograph was taken. 5 November 1965

4-6-0 No 6923 Croxteth Hall *in steam at 82E Bristol Barrow Road, just one week before closure. 14 November 1965*

Class 3 2-6-2T No 82030 in the yard at 82F Bath Green Park. This was the last Western Region shed to maintain steam, finally closing in March 1966. 14 November 1965.

Crewe Works had plenty of steam locos present and still had four years of repairs to steam ahead of it. Ninety-five engines were to be seen, but a sign of the times showed up in the lack of ex LMS passenger engine power with only one "Jubilee" No 45583 *Assam* being repaired. By contrast, Nos 46103 *Royal Scots Fusilier,* 46119 *Lancashire Fusilier,* 46130 *The West Yorkshire Regiment,* 46145 *The Duke of Wellington's Regiment (West Riding)* and 46252 *City of Leicester* were in various stages of being cut up.

A day trip to York in late October was followed by a Warwickshire Railway Society tour of the Glasgow and Edinburgh sheds in late November. We travelled overnight by service train and on arrival at Glasgow (Central) we joined our mode of transport for the day, a fleet of buses. It was "plastic mac" weather, one of those atrociously cold, misty days with constant rain, a nightmare one for jotting down numbers. Sheds visited were Corkerhill, Dawsholm, Eastfield, Kipps, Motherwell, Parkhead, Polmadie and St. Rollox in and around Glasgow, Dalry Road, Haymarket and St. Margarets in Edinburgh and finally Bathgate.

Although large numbers of steam were seen at these depots, the ranks of stored ones almost outnumbered the active locos, nowhere more so than at Bathgate. Out of a total of forty steam, thirty-two were on the dump but, unlike my visit of 1962, many of the stored engines were "Pacifics", these being Nos 60057 *Ormonde,* 60087 *Blenheim,* 60089 *Felstead,* 60098 *Spion Kop,* 60099 *Call Boy,* 60101 *Cicero,* 60159 *Bonnie Dundee,* 60529 *Pearl Diver,* 60534 *Irish Elegance* and 60537 *Bachelor's Button.*

During the course of the trip a further dozen or so named passenger locos were observed in store with about the same number of active ones noted, many from English depots. It certainly looked as though the scene was set for the early disappearance of Scottish based "Pacific" engine power. However, for a change, steam was to fight back and Dalry Road shed contained the first clues as to this minor miracle. Amongst the total of twenty-four steam there were three A4s, one was Scottish, No 60024 *Kingfisher,* but the other two were from New England (Peterborough) Nos 60006 *Sir Ralph Wedgwood* and 60007 *Sir Nigel Gresley,* and at the time no-one in our party could explain their presence. They turned out to be the advance vanguard of nine members of the class transferred from England to supplement the Scottish based members and were used on the upgraded Aberdeen-Glasgow services on which some survived until late 1966. The seven sister engines transferred were Nos 60005 *Sir Charles Newton,* 60010 *Dominion of Canada,* 60016 *Silver King,* 60019 *Bittern,* 60023 *Golden Eagle,* 60026 *Miles Beevor* and 60034 *Lord Faringdon.*

After this trip I joined the Bromford Loco Society, a club similar to the REC which again did shed visits by coach. As a finale to 1963 I went with them in early December to East Anglia calling in at Woodford Halse, March, New England, Wellingborough, Leicester G.C., Leicester (Midland) and Nuneaton. At March shed steam was well on the retreat

Class 4 2-6-4T No 42462 in the yard at 8F Springs Branch, Wigan. 21 November 1965

'Flying Pig' 2-6-0 No 43019 at 10H Lower Darwen. This shed contrary to most was at the top of a hill on the approach from one side. 21 November 1965

with only twenty-three examples of which eight were "Britannias" Nos 70002 *Geoffrey Chaucer,* 70003 *John Bunyan,* 70007 *Coeur-de-Lion,* 70008 *Black Prince,* 70009 *Alfred the Great,* 70011 *Hotspur,* 70013 *Oliver Cromwell* and 70035 *Rudyard Kipling.* All of these were destined shortly to go to Carlisle and soon after our visit the shed closed to steam.

At New England, despite the ban on steam south of Peterborough, there was still plenty to be seen. A variety of ex LMS engines were observed, mostly 'foreigners' and eleven "Pacifics" were among the total of sixty-seven steam. Five A4s stood forlornly in store, condemned and unwanted even by the Scottish region, Nos 60017 *Silver Fox,* 60021 *Wild Swan,* 60025 *Falcon,* 60029 *Woodcock* and 60032 *Gannet.* By contrast, five clean A3s and an A1 were active on the shed, Nos 60054 *Prince of Wales,* 60062 *Minoru,* 60063 *Isinglass,* 60065 *Knight of Thistle,* 60106 *Flying Fox* and 60149 *Amadis.* Most of these were living on borrowed time and all would be withdrawn by the end of the following year.

So ended 1963, and with similar mass withdrawals to 1962, the outlook for the remaining BR steam was looking bleak. I observed 2634 steam locos during the year on thirty various trips.

1964

When 1964 arrived steam was very much on the retreat and in many parts of Britain it had disappeared for ever, helped by the fact that the Beeching Axe was forcing many lines to be closed. Because of these factors my visits to sheds increased during the year in a desperate race against time to see as many steam locos as possible before they were withdrawn. Lack of space compels me to gloss over many of these shed visits and instead I will concentrate on various other matters of interest to the railway fraternity.

The year began for Baz and myself in January with a rail trip to York and Darlington behind "Britannia", No 70000 *Britannia* herself. A remarkable sight on York shed was A1 No 60120 *Kittiwake* with a badly damaged front bufferbeam and main frame. This was the result of a collision with a mail train a few hours before, as the loco was still in steam, needless to say it was condemned the same day.

On arrival at Darlington a fleet of buses was waiting to ferry us to the shed, works and scrapyard. As our bus negotiated a corner on the road bridge someone on the top deck shouted "A train's coming", consequently all the passengers on the one side rushed across to the other so as not to miss it. The timing of the rush coincided unfortunately with the bus being at its tightest curve of turning having the effect of upsetting the centre of gravity, making the bus rock alarmingly. The driver was not very impressed either for he stopped and came upstairs, but as we were back in our seats as if nothing had happened, he could do little more than glare at us and mutter under his breath.

On my next trip, a Sunday in February, by rail to Liverpool with Baz and three other friends, one of the most amusing incidents during my spotter's years occurred. After visiting Aintree shed we returned to the main road and after consulting the timetable found we had twenty minutes or so to wait for a bus to take us to the city centre. Fortunately the bus stop was outside a conveniently open pub, and we took it in turns to keep a watch for the bus. It fell to the unfortunate Baz to be outside when it came into sight, and hurriedly finishing our drinks we rushed outside. It was one of the old buses with an open platform and vertical pole and we almost missed it, for as we arrived it started to move. Baz stood on one side to let us on and I made my way upstairs. After sitting down I heard a peculiar pitterpattering from downstairs and the sound of ever-increasing laughter. I returned to the bottom deck and was confronted by one of the funniest sights I have ever seen. Baz had tried to get on the bus but its acceleration had reached the point where he was too frightened to jump on or to let go. So there he was, hanging on for grim death with his speed increasing as the driver changed through the gears. By now he was quite red in the face. Being a little

overweight and not exactly 100 per cent fit did not help. We tried, between bouts of helpless laughter to help him but to no avail. Whilst all this was going on the conductor and other passengers were dumbstruck, consequently nobody attempted to ring the bell to stop the bus.

Poor old Baz must have accompanied the bus in this way for a quarter of a mile. To add to his general discomfort and our continued mirth, as the bus crossed a main street there were twenty or so people waiting at another bus stop, and upon seeing Baz run past complete with bus they started to point at him and collapse with laughter. Shortly after, the bus stopped and we were able to carry Baz aboard, whereupon the conductor duly asked him for full fare!

Not many locos of particular interest were seen that day and at Edge Hill there were only four reminders of the depot's once proud passenger steam fleet, "Coronations" Nos 46229 *Duchess of Hamilton,* 46233 *Duchess of Sutherland,* 46241 *City of Edinburgh* and 46243 *City of Lancaster,* the first two in store.

Class J27 0-6-0 No 65832 in steam inside the straight shed at 52G Sunderland. 28 November 1965

Two coach trips with the Bromford Society to sheds in London and South Wales produced a total of nearly 1000 steam and it was during the course of the latter journey that I began to realise why Baz was a little more than overweight. Most of us had a few sandwiches or rolls for sustenance, but not Baz. He used to bring a large biscuit tin crammed so full of goodies that a large rubber band had to be used to hold the lid on.

At the beginning of April, I applied for and succeeded in getting a job as a signalbox lad and was posted to Barnt Green on the Midland line from Birmingham to Bristol. I worked there until September and enjoyed it immensely. Though the regular expresses were rostered for diesels there were many failures with "Black 5s" and "Jubilees" substituting. Most freights were steam hauled and during the summer service many of the holiday extras were also in steam hands, often B1 4-6-0s from the Eastern Region. One particular memory was of a MR 0-6-0 at the head of a heavy summer extra after toiling up the Lickey incline.

The month of May saw us visiting the sheds in southern England and in June I went by rail to Barnstaple, where the line from Taunton was one of the last bastions of the old GWR 53XX 2-6-0s. In early July, Baz and I, and two other friends, Wilb and Lanks set off on our mopeds for an overnight tour of the Peak District. After visiting Stafford shed we pressed on to Uttoxeter. The shed was in the middle of nowhere and apparently served little purpose. Crossing a barren field in pitch darkness Lanks disappeared down a large hole. He was a big bloke but fortunately only his pride was hurt.

By now it was 3.00am and for July very cold. We headed for Buxton and after getting lost eventually arrived at 6.00am by which time we were like brass monkeys. After doing the shed we had over two hours to wait for a cafe to open. The time dragged so slowly it nearly put us off such trips for life. Whilst hanging around Buxton station a BR permanent way crew rolled up in a truck and their first priority was to lift the biggest and most antiquated kettle we had ever seen off their wagon. It looked as though it was constructed from iron and was filthy dirty. But we would have given anything for the chance of a steaming cuppa!

'MOST OF US HAD A FEW SANDWICHES FOR SUSTENANCE, BUT NOT BAZ . . . WE BEGAN TO REALISE WHY HE WAS A LITTLE OVERWEIGHT . . .'

After thawing out at a "Mr Kipling" type cafe run by a Chinaman with a perfect north country accent, we moved on to Stoke and finally Oxley where we were astounded to find ten "Castles" on shed most of which were in steam Nos 5000 *Launceston Castle,* 5026 *Criccieth Castle,* 5063 *Earl Baldwin,* 5089 *Westminster Castle,* 7005 *Sir Edward Elgar,* 7011 *Banbury Castle,* 7012 *Barry Castle,* 7014 *Caerhays Castle,* 7023 *Penrice Castle,* and 7024 *Powis Castle.* Never again would we witness such a noble gathering.

After recovering from this trip Baz and I set off once again on an ambitious overnight moped journey in late July to Doncaster. We started in the late afternoon and visited Coalville, Overseal, Burton, Nottingham and Toton before arriving at Colwick around midnight. We passed the main entrance, parked our mopeds and slipped into the shed through some conveniently missing bars in a metal fence.

After negotiating the depot on our way out imminent disaster overtook us in the shape of the foreman. Baz had by now developed a confident attitude towards those in authority which had got us out of many predicaments and he always had a string of excuses and ficticious explanations to hand. Upon being asked what we were doing there and why hadn't we called in at the main office, Baz replied that we hadn't seen it. The foreman then said: "You cannot miss it, its all lit up". Baz persisted with the excuse, but the chap was not to be budged and it looked as if he was about to call the police.

0-6-0 No 1948 in Darling Harbour yard, in the centre of Sydney, Australia. These ancient machines were used for shunting and the author spent a great deal of time on the footplate of this and its sister engines whilst working as a shunter. June 1966

Another foreman-type joined us and asked his colleague what was happening. He then turned to us and asked which direction we had come from. Baz pointed leftwards saying, "That direction, from Annesley", to which the second foreman, a twinkle in his eye, quick as a flash replied: "Oh, have you indeed. It's a pity it is the end of a cul-de-sac in that direction. What have you got to say about that then?". Baz was flabbergasted and lost for words. Fortunately the second chap had a sense of humour and let us leave the depot without further ado.

After this narrow escape we headed for Annesley with its nearby overhead coal bucket system from a mine. These things were permanently on the move and in the darkness their constant squeaking and groaning made one more nervous than usual, thinking that 'authority' was on hand. Between Langwith and Retford the dawn arrived and as we motored sedately along the main road we noticed that we were accompanied by hundreds of rabbits running alongside, we nicknamed then the "Bawtry Bunnies". Shortly afterwards we stopped for breakfast and Baz produced of all things an obnoxious box of faggots.

The rest of the day passed without incident with Retford, Doncaster, Mexborough, Canklow, Wath, Darnall, Hasland and Staveley sheds visited.

For the first week in August we went on a repeat tour of Scotland on similar lines to the one I had been on in 1962. Despite the ever increasing dieselisation it was surprising how much steam was still active, I saw only 300 or so less than on the first holiday and one highlight was being hauled throughout from Crewe to Carlisle behind "Britannia" No 70035 *Rudyard Kipling* and breasting Shap summit unaided.

After returning from Scotland, the remainder of August and early September saw trips to Liverpool, London, Isle of Wight and Rhyl. In late September I was offered the chance of a signal box job at Hatton, between Birmingham and Paddington. I reluctantly left Barnt Green box, and the signalman whom I had worked with for several months was later destined to become my stepfather.

So I moved on to pastures new and duly reported to Hatton Station. Apart from the main line it was a junction for Stratford and boasted three signalboxes, South, North and West, of which mine was to be the latter, a class four, the lowest of the low. Barnt Green had been a spacious, modern and busy box with all mod cons. I knew I had to start at the bottom of the ladder but Hatton West must have fallen off it; it would have looked old even in a museum! It had a toilet of sorts, a small detached Nissen hut affair, the last customer of which had probably been a baled-out German pilot, it was so antiquated. The box's most modern amenity, apart from the roof, was a small coal fire. There was no electricity and the only means of lighting was an ancient device fueled by methylated spirits and compressed air, for which a bicycle pump was supplied. The sole cooking facility was a primus stove, and water for the kettle was obtained from a stream one hundred yards down the track, and it constantly clogged the kettle with lime. The box was not very busy but it did at least control a double track junction; thus the scene was set for my new career.

There were three other trainees and we spent a lot of time learning the rules, instructed by an experienced signalman. Occasionally when the stationmaster was away we would be summoned to Hatton South for a clandestine game of cards. These sessions passed peacefully until the day the stationmaster returned early. He was not spotted until he was on the footbridge and as the main exit from the box was adjacent to it we panicked and leapt out of the windows before returning to our respective boxes through nearby undergrowth.

4-6-0 No 3020 in steam at Rozelle yard, New South Wales, Australia in June 1966. Loco built by Beyer Peacock, Manchester.

As nothing was mentioned for several days we thought we had got away with it, until out of the blue the stationmaster said to us rather dryly: "Next time you leave the box why don't you try the stairs, the railway went to a great deal of time and trouble to get them installed". He did not mention anything about card playing, but must have suspected what had been going on.

In November I passed my rules and became a fully fledged class four signalman, but I was to stay at Hatton for only a short while.

To return to the spotting scene, the Bromford Society had folded up but Baz and I joined yet another one from Walsall, enabling us to continue on coach trips. Venues until the end of 1964 were East Anglia, Manchester, Bournemouth and Blackpool. All passed without incident except on the latter when, travelling home by rail, I was stranded at Preston during the early hours after missing my connection and was nearly arrested as a vagrant.

A highly successful year's spotting came to an end in which 6164 steam locos had been noted, the highest ever.

The end of the road at 2B Oxley. The shed had been closed but housed a few stored locos. At the forefront Class 3 2-6-0 No 46428 destined for Barry Docks, and later for preservation at Strathspey Railway, albeit for spare parts. 29 May 1967

Steam to spare at 9B Stockport. In the centre 9F Class 2-10-0 No 92234. 8 January 1967

Run Down of Steam

1965-1966

1965

The year began with still quite a large steam fleet but it was to be a different story by the time the year drew to a close, with steam all but gone from the Eastern and Western Regions.

I had been a signalman at Hatton for less than two months when I was offered a class three job at Earlswood Lakes on the North Warwickshire line, this was indeed rapid advancement. It was larger and more modern than Hatton West, being supplied with electricity. But there was still no toilet and water was delivered in milk churns! During the winter service steam was restricted to freight workings, but I was lucky enough to be working on a line still served by a variety of the remaining types of ex-GWR engines.

Spotting-wise the year started with a coach trip to the Gloucester, Bristol and Swindon areas in January, soon followed by a special train hauled by "Britannia" No 70042 *Lord Roberts* from Birmingham to Crewe, where both sheds and the works were visited. Crewe (North) held thirty-two steam, but with the exception of a solitary "Royal Scot" No 46115 *Scots Guardsman* from Kingmoor and three stored "Jubilees", all vestige of LMS passenger engine power had gone. In its place were sixteen "Britannias" and a visiting "Clan" No 72005 *Clan MacGregor,* again of Kingmoor. Out of 181 steam locos we saw during the day the total of "Britannias" came to an amazing twenty-four.

It was not long before I passed out for Earlswood box and for some months worked twelve hours days and nights on alternate weeks. With the extra money I had been able to buy myself a 200cc Triumph Tiger Cub motor bike. In early April Baz and I used it for a tour of the Manchester sheds in which we covered 350 miles. It is not surprising that with our combined weight, eventually the bike overheated and we had a struggle to get home.

A few days later saw us on a coach trip to the Eastern counties visiting Frodingham, Hull, Goole, York, Doncaster and Retford sheds. Amongst the total of thirty-three steam at Hull (Dairycoates), nine were destined for Drapers scrapyard and oblivion, two of them being "Jubilee" No 45597 *Barbados* and A1 No 60126 *Sir Vincent Raven.* Doncaster was not the force it had been but steam was still well represented with forty-six examples. A pleasant sight on this shed was an A1 from York No 60145 *Saint Mungo* and, destined to be the last example of LNER "Pacific" power based in England, surviving until June 1966.

In many parts of the country, there were by mid 1965, few depots where you could see active steam in double figures, let alone in large numbers. In

4-6-0 No 7029 Clun Castle *shunting empty stock at Chester after arrival from Banbury with the first of two specials marking the end of through services between Paddington and Birkenhead. 4 March 1967*

4-6-0 No 4079 Pendennis Castle *arrives at Chester with the second special on 4 March 1967. Note LNWR gantry. The locomotive is now preserved in Australia.*

June Lanks and I went on a three-day tour on his motor bike and many sheds visited were either devoid of steam or not far off closure. Kirkby, Langwith and Staveley GC were all poorly represented, the latter shed was in a sad state of repair and the nearby rows of terraced houses were all but derelict. Barrow Hill was a little brighter with twenty-nine steam and at Wath diesel/electric depot we were surprised to see a steam trespasser 8F 2-8-0 No 48092 simmering gently in the yard.

On then to Royston (nineteen steam) and Wakefield, still a steam bastion, held fifty locos, thirty-two of them WD 2-8-0s. Manningham was down to just eight steam examples; out of Skipton's twenty-four locos, ten were in store and Hellifield was closed. Tebay had only three locos on show, but a few others must have been on banking duties.

Carlisle (Upperby) was a pale shadow compared to my previous visit in August 1964 when out of forty-six locos, twenty-four were named including nine "Coronations". Twenty-two of these named locos were: Nos 45512 *Bunsen,* 45526 *Morecambe and Heysham,* 45527 *Southport,* 45532 *Illustrious,* 45545 *Planet,* 45595 *Southern Rhodesia,* 45640 *Frobisher,* 45703 *Thunderer,* 45716 *Swiftsure,* 45742 *Connaught,* 46110 *Grenadier Guardsman,* 46118 *Royal Welsh Fusilier,* 46200 *The Princess Royal* (stored for almost two years), 46225 *Duchess of Gloucester,* 46226 *Duchess of Norfolk,* 46235 *City of Birmingham,* 46237 *City of Bristol,* 46241 *City of Edinburgh,* 46244 *King George VI,* 46250 *City of Lichfield,* 46251 *City of Nottingham* and 46256 *Sir William A. Stanier F.R.S.* All of these latter engines, were now gone, never to be seen again in service.

Kingmoor was its usual reliable self with fifty-two steam and many of the surviving "Patriots", "Jubilees" and "Royal Scots" allocated here, but few in active service.

Workington was a stronghold of the few remaining "Duck" Class 6 0-6-0s and twelve were observed out of twenty locos. Barrow again had a poor showing with only fourteen steam. We turned southwards and for home calling at Carnforth, Lancaster and Lostock Hall sheds, none of which held large numbers of locos.

At the commencement of the summer service, the steam hauled freights along the North Warwicks were enhanced by the appearance of some steam powered holiday expresses to resorts in Devon. Mostly in the hands of ex GWR 4-6-0s they were supported by LMS "Black 5s" and "Britannias" and for several months were a welcome addition.

Whilst I was at Earlswood one or two interesting incidents occurred. Until the demise of the freight services towards the end of the year, the box was open twenty-four hours a day, except Sundays, unless there were diversions. At night, the nearest boxes open were at Tyseley, towards Birmingham, and Bearley near to Stratford. Earlswood itself was at the top of an incline from both directions, the one from Bearley being the furthest and stiffest climb, which from time to time required the assistance of a banker. On average, a freight passing Bearley would take around fifty minutes to reach Earlswood.

One particular night, nearly an hour had passed with no sound or sight of a freight from Bearley and I was contemplating stopping a Stratford bound train, which was due, when I heard the faint chugging of a steam loco coming from the Stratford direction. My mind at rest, I let the other freight go by unhindered. However as the minutes ticked by, all was silent again and I began to wish I had stopped the other freight and asked the driver to keep a lookout.

Before deciding on further action I spotted a light from a handlamp in the distance. Much to my relief, its owner was the driver of the missing freight which had run short of steam about a mile away and he had left his fireman to make amends. He was obviously not happy with his loco, as before he left the box he said in a lilting Welsh accent: "Bloody steam engines, I'm on the Margam tomorrow and thank goodness I've got a diesel". Eventually enough steam was raised and the train cleared my section.

The following day, sure enough, there he was giving me a cheery wave as he passed by comfortably seated in the cab of a Brush Type 4 diesel. He did not smile for long though; before his train reached Tyseley the brakes on the loco seized and he was stranded again. I would liked to have heard his comments.

Despite the lack of attention and general run down of the surviving members of the WR steam fleet I rarely had a failure or many examples of having to set trains back into the sidings for a "blow up." Despite the fact that many of these engine crews were shortly to lose their jobs, I must pay tribute to the way in which the majority attempted to keep right time with their run-down charges. Redundancy was a poor reward for their efforts.

As a rule, on nights, after the last passenger train had gone around midnight, nothing was booked to use the line for about two hours. On one such shift I had an urgent need for a call of nature and as there was no toilet in the box it meant using the one on the station. As I anticipated being away from the box for only a short while, I neglected to inform the other signalman of my absence.

A large notice on the door stated "Out of Use," but my needs by now were quite desperate and thinking the notice would only affect the general public I chose to ignore it. On attempting to leave the cubicle I found out why it was out of use — there was no handle on the inside of the very solid door, which was firmly shut. The nearest house was some distance away and I banged and shouted to no avail, soon giving it up as a waste of time. Being an old building, the ceiling was about fifteen feet off the ground. The only way I could get out of my predicament would be to climb onto the cistern and somehow clamber over the top of the inside toilet wall which had thoughtfully been provided with long spikes.

The other alternative was to stay there until help arrived. This help would have undoubtedly been an inspector summoned by my colleagues when unable to contact me in the signalbox. As I could not face the embarrassment and humiliation of being rescued in this way I chose the former method to try and escape. It was extremely difficult and harrowing, the cistern just about took my weight and I had visions of falling into the pan. I had to squeeze between the spikes and ceiling; all it needed was one slip to ruin my chances of one day becoming a father.

Having got over this obstacle I then faced the difficulty of reaching the ground, a rather long drop. Keeping a tentative hold on the spikes was not easy as my hands were wet with fear but gradually I was able to work my way round until I reached something solid to stand on before jumping down. With great relief I slunk back to the safety of the signalbox.

At the end of July I went on my motor bike to some sheds in South Wales to find that steam was all but finished. Severn Tunnel Junction had twenty-five steam occupants, mostly dead or stored engines. The surviving 2-6-2 tanks which had for countless years assisted freights in and out of the tunnel were cold and silent Nos 4107/10/15/21/44/56/57/60 and 6144. Some were however, destined for Barry scrapyard and preservation in later years, so all was not lost to the cutter's torch. At Cardiff (Radyr) steam was finished, its eleven remaining occupants standing forlornly buffer to buffer in three rows shorn of numberplates. Four years previously, on a trip with the REC, forty-six steam locos were present, all in service and after going round the shed some of us were caught by the foreman who demanded to know who was in charge. As our leader had stayed on the coach everyone the foreman asked pointed to someone else in the party. This made him rather wild and he ordered one of his underlings to call the police. At this point we fled down the yard pursued by the foreman and several others, but as we were younger and fitter we reached the coach and were away well before they arrived.

Newport (Ebbw Junction) did at least have some live steam but the depot was reduced to a mere twenty-five, some of which were strangers from the Midlands. Gloucester (Horton Road) again had twenty-five steam on shed including the last remaining "Castle" in service No 7029 *Clun Castle.*

The following Sunday, in early August, I went with Lanks on his motor bike to the Leeds area. Many of the sheds we visited were still very active and some were to continue with steam for another two years. Royston was visited first, followed by Wakefield, this imposing depot landmarked by nearby cooling towers contained a formidable total of eighty-three steam. From Wakefield we went to Ardsley which still contained four A1s, alas three of which were condemned, and in store Nos 60117 *Bois Roussel,* 60133 *Pommern* and 60148 *Aboyeur.* The fourth, No 60130 *Kestrel,* survived until the shed closed in October. Out of thirteen B1 4-6-0s, six were named, Nos 61013 *Topi,* 61017 *Bushbuck,* 61030 *Nyala,* 61237 *Geoffrey H. Kitson,* 61238 *Leslie Runciman* and 61240 *Harry Hinchcliffe.* If these latter three were named after high-ups on the railway, they were not very inspiring. In fact I always thought of them as being names of comperes at working mens' clubs.

On to Leeds itself, where at Neville Hill we found four working A1s Nos 60118 *Archibald Sturrock,* 60131 *Osprey,* 60134 *Foxhunter* and 60154 *Bon Accord.* Like *Kestrel* at Ardsley, their working lives to would end in

October. At Holbeck forty-three steam were seen, nineteen of them "Black 5s", but present to brighten the place up were six "Jubilees" Nos 45573 *Newfoundland,* 45608 *Gibraltar,* 45626 *Seychelles,* 45658 *Keyes,* 45675 *Hardy* and 45697 *Archilles.*

Moving on from Leeds we visited Stourton, Wath, Tinsley and Staveley (Barrow Hill) before reaching our final shed at Langwith.

During the year I had passed my driving test and before my next trip in September had purchased a 'sit up and beg' Ford motor car off my brother-in-law for the princely sum of £20. It did not last for long as it was rather old and eventually seized up, but not before I used it on a marathon two day tour. The "Twelve Counties Tour" as I nicknamed it, after passing through the counties of Warwickshire, Staffordshire, Cheshire, Lancashire, Westmorland, Cumberland, Northumberland, Durham, Yorkshire, Nottinghamshire, Derbyshire and Leicestershire. Those were in the days when counties were real ones not like the artifical West Midlands and Strathclyde of today. I covered 625 miles and visited seventeen sheds — Stafford, Stoke, Carnforth, Tebay, Carlisle (Upperby and Kingmoor) Blaydon, Gateshead, West Hartlepool, Thornaby, York, Hull, Doncaster, Wath, Kirkby, Colwick and Toton and noted 398 steam to 280 diesels.

Out of these sheds Carlisle (Kingmoor) had the largest steam representation, seventy-eight, of which thirty-eight were "Black 5s". Present were the four surviving "Patriots" and "Royal Scots" Nos 45530 *Sir Frank Ree,* 45531 *Sir Frederick Harrison,* 46115 *Scots Guardsman* and 46140 *King's Royal Rifle Corps.* A notable visitor was A3 No 60041 *Salmon Trout* of St. Margarets (Edinburgh). Between the two Carlisle sheds they also mustered nineteen "Britannias" and three "Clans".

One of the saddest sights on this tour was that of Toton with its massive roundhouses all but devoid of steam, only twenty locos on shed, some of which were stored.

In November all freights on the North Warwickshire line ceased and rumours became rife about the closure of the line. The future, job-wise, became bleak and in a fit of youthful impetuosity I made arrangements to emigrate to Australia. As I was not going to depart until early 1966 I made up my mind to visit as many of the remaining steam sheds that I could in the time available.

I went on four coach trips with the Walsall Loco Club in November and December. The first was to some of the remaining WR steam sheds in England: Worcester, Gloucester (Horton Road), Bristol (Barrow Road), Bath (Green Park), Swindon and Oxford. Of these Oxford was truly the last bastion of ex GWR steam with seven 2-6-2 tanks and no less than seventeen named 4-6-0s gathered: Nos 4920 *Dumbleton Hall,* 4962 *Ragley Hall,* 6815 *Frilford Grange,* 6868 *Penrhos Grange,* 6874 *Haughton Grange,*

6910 *Gossington Hall*, 6921 *Borwick Hall*, 6927 *Lilford Hall*, 6931 *Aldborough Hall*, 6977 *Helmington Hall*, 6953 *Leighton Hall*, 6957 *Norcliffe Hall*, 6959 *Peatling Hall*, 6961 *Stedham Hall*, 6967 *Willesley Hall*, 7909 *Heveningham Hall* and 7922 *Salford Hall*. Though shorn of names and numberplates many were still in service and apart from a smattering of ex-GWR locos seen again at the end of 1966 and beginning of 1967, this was to be the last time I would see the engines I had grown up with.

The remaining three trips were to depots in the North West and North East of England, but before leaving the railway and departing for Australia I had a final fling on my own. I had a soft spot for the Waterloo-Bournemouth line and wanted also to travel behind steam. On New Year's Eve, the outward run was via Salisbury, as I wanted to visit the shed there, unfortunately being hauled by a "Warship" diesel. I travelled to Southampton on a multiple unit and was pulled by rebuilt "West Country" No 34101 *Hartland* to Bournemouth. After doing the shed I returned to Waterloo behind "Merchant Navy" No 35017 *Belgian Marine*.

Whilst still in London I visited Nine Elms where out of forty-two steam locos, nineteen were "Pacifics", Nos 34001 *Exeter*, 34002 *Salisbury*, 34004 *Yeovil*, 34005 *Barnstaple*, 34007 *Wadebridge*, 34009 *Lyme Regis*, 34032

Almost the end for Southern steam. BR Class 5 4-6-0 No 73020, with home-made front number plate, in steam at 70F Bournemouth. 21 May 1967

Camelford, 34033 *Chard,* 34034 *Honiton,* 34038 *Braunton,* 34104 *Bere Alston,* 34108 *Wincanton,* 35007 *Aberdeen Commonwealth,* 35011 *General Steam Navigation,* 35017 *Belgian Marine,* 35023 *Holland Afrika Line,* 35026 *Lamport and Holt Line,* 35027 *Port Line* and 35030 *Elder Dempster Lines.* Unlike the other regions the Southern still seemed to have a certain amount of pride in its steam allocation and the majority still proudly carried nameplates. Apart from the "Britannias", never again was I to see such a majestic gathering of steam passenger locos in one place.

So ended 1965 in which I had seen nearly 4700 steam locos. At the time I presumed they would be the last I would ever see again in Britain.

1966

I left England during January and flew to Sydney. I had a rather unhappy time in Australia, suffered a lot of home-sickness and was almost called up as a National Serviceman in the Australian army, which at the time was fighting alongside the Americans in Vietnam. After a few months I came back home.

The only bright feature about my stay in Australia was that New South Wales had plenty of steam the majority of which was conveniently concentrated in Sydney. I worked in various jobs on the railway, first as a loco cleaner, then a parcels porter at the main Sydney station and finally as a shunter. The steam classes varied from small crane tanks right up the scale to the large 38 Class "Pacifics" and Class 60 4-8-4 + 4-8-4 Beyer Garretts which were constructed around 1952-54. It was a pleasure to be involved with these locos and altogether I saw 195 different ones.

I arrived back in England in October, jobless, penniless but thankful to be home. I tried to rejoin the railway but more jobs were being lost than created and I was unsuccessful. Baz and I met up again and soon we were out on the road again on bigger and better trips than before. He had now progressed to owning a car himself, a Ford 100E. I was by a quirk of fate reduced to riding around on the old moped I had parted company with in early 1965 when I had sold it to my stepfather, never having thought it would still be going strong two years later.

The steam situation in Britain had not changed a great deal in the short time I had been away. The ER had lost its allocation along with the WR which was expected anyway, and the only major events had been the closure of most of the old Great Central resulting in the demise of Annesley and the Somerset & Dorset Lines.

After my early disappointment of not being able to rejoin the railway, I soon found alternative employment. Whilst I began to acquire some sort of spending money Baz and I restricted our spotting activities to local sheds. Steam was very much on the way out in the Birmingham area with Tyseley closed to steam in November and Saltley and Oxley soon to follow early in 1967.

Another shot of 70F Bournemouth with Class 4 4-6-0 No 75075, without front number plate, in steam. 21 May 1967.

Line up of locos at 5B Crewe (South). The three main locos (l. to r.) 'Britannia' No 70023 Venus, *8F 2-8-0's Nos 48474 and 48436. 29 May 1967*

Alongside the shed building at 5B Crewe (South). Main loco is 8F 2-8-0 No 48767. 29 May 1967.

The Fires are Drawn
1967-1968

From 1967 until the end of steam Baz and I covered many thousands of miles by car. At first we travelled alone but later on we were accompanied by other friends. We had more humorous incidents during the last twenty months of steam than in many of the previous years put together. Baz and I had over the years adopted very successful methods of bunking sheds. We either went round in a flash or took our time and kept in the shadows, depending on the circumstances, taking care to steer clear of offices and open yards. Despite trying constantly to drum this into our companions as the recipe for success, on occasions they would forget and get us into deep water. Nevertheless our success rate for getting round sheds was phenomenal, and we still look back on those times with justifiable pride.

My role became the usual one of planning the trips, with Baz as the anchor man for excuses. 1967 started in the right spirit with a mammoth trip to the North West as far as Carlisle, across to Newcastle and down to the Leeds, Sheffield, Manchester and Nottingham areas, all in three days. I planned everything down to the last detail, or so I thought, working out the mileage between depots and how long it would take. I forgot to take into account road conditions, weather, eating time or even stopping for sleep. Consequently within the first twenty-four hours we were twelve hours behind my schedule.

The trip was littered with mishaps and bad luck. It snowed almost constantly and in Chester we stopped to assist a car owner who was stranded, unable to start his car. During the time we were pushing the car, disaster prone Baz slipped and disappeared underneath it into a pile of slush. He was uncomfortable for some time after. We visited the Liverpool sheds and slowly made our way north calling in at various depots on the way. How we made it to the top of Shap on the old A6 road at night and in a blizzard I will never know.

By the time we reached Carlisle we were so far behind schedule that we skipped the North East part of it and cut off down to Leeds. By this time it was late evening and we got lost looking for Holbeck shed, so we stopped and asked a pedestrian for directions. Unfortunately he was drunk, and after muttering incoherently, fell against the side of the car, slid down the side onto the bonnet and into the gutter.

Steam seen on Wakefield shed proved to be one of the highlights of this trip. It was packed to the brim with eighty-six engines, many of them visitors from sheds as far away as Liverpool. After going round I stood by one of the braziers to have a smoke and warm myself up and I remember with nostalgia looking across the rows of engines at one end of the depot building, all simmering away gently, with steam and smoke being reflected by the yard lights. All seemed so tranquil as if the threat to steam was a million years away. Yet in six months the shed would be dead.

After completing the sheds in the area we made for Manchester, but in the wilds of one of the passes the weather and road conditions became so

BR Class 9F 2-10-0 No 92220 Evening Star *ex Works in the paint shop at Crewe. 29 May 1967. We made our way unofficially around the Works on this occasion until our nerve cracked at the sight of increasing numbers of bowler-hatted gentlemen!*

Spotters' eye view of 5D Stoke from the inside. Nearest loco is 8F 2-8-0 No 48256. 29 May 1967

Class 5 4-6-0 No 45052 in the yard at 5D Stoke. 29 May 1967

bad we pulled into a lay-by for some sleep. Not long after we settled down one of the doors burst open, frightening the life out of us. A torch was shone, held by one of two police officers who demanded to know 'who we were; where had we been; where were we going and what were we doing in the middle of nowhere on such a foul night?' When we explained that we were trainspotting they gave us the impression we were off our rockers, but eventually our identities were established and they went on their way.

The next day we descended into Manchester and did all the sheds before moving on to Nottingham and returning home. It was a good trip and we saw 881 steam locos, almost one for every mile travelled, and both Baz and I virtually finished off the remaining locos we still needed.

A trip to East Anglia in February was followed, for myself, with a steam special. On the 4 March two specials were run from Paddington-Birkenhead behind two "Castles" from Banbury-Chester, as a final gesture before the through trains were withdrawn from this route, reducing the once proud Snow Hill to a secondary role. I travelled on the first train behind No 7029 *Clun Castle*, the second one following behind with No 4079 *Pendennis Castle*. On the return from Chester I terminated my journey at Snow Hill, where I bade farewell not only to *Clun Castle* but also to one of my favourite stations which had given me so much pleasure. over the years. I never set foot in it again.

In early April we visited the Sheffield and Nottingham areas again. I had by now obtained another car, an old but extremely reliable Austin A50, and used it in turns with Baz's car on trips. During the course of this particular trip we were again apprehended by a foreman at Colwick. We had already

Filth and grime. The epitome of a loco shed yard in the closing days of steam. 5D Stoke only two months off closure. Class 5 4-6-0 No 45241 in view. 29 May 1967

10A Carnforth was one of the last bastions of steam. This shot of the north end of the shed was enhanced by (l. to r.) "Jubilee" 4-6-0 No 45675 Hardy, *and No 45562* Alberta. *'Britannia' 4-6-2 No 70010* Owen Glendower *and 8F 2-8-0 No 48252. All of these were from other depots. 17 June 1967*

9F Class 2-10-0 No 92108 in steam at 10A Carnforth north end yard. 17 June 1967

been round the shed and were wary of a repeat performance of the fiasco in 1964 and were surprised when the foreman offered us a guide. We obviously couldn't tell him that we had already been round, so had to suffer in silence with a guide who must have been the oldest chap at the depot, who walked at no more than a snail's pace. Still, we were grateful for small mercies.

In mid-May we went on a two-day tour of the West Country and to a handful of Southern depots, the latter being the only ones where we saw live steam. Whilst at Eastleigh we decided to have a crack at the Works. We came across a small gap in some railings and, being short and slim of build I was able to slip through easily. Not so Baz; try as he did he found it impossible and at one stage was stuck fast. I left him on the other side of the fence, nipped round the works and on my return found him rather subdued and ruefully regretting the days he had eaten too much.

The last shed we visited was at Salisbury, which turned out to be the last time we were to see Southern "Pacifics" in steam, as they were all to be withdrawn in July. Although by now devoid of nameplates they still had a high standard of cleanliness and five examples were on shed, Nos 34006 *Bude,* 34013 *Okehampton,* 34052 *Lord Dowding,* 34089 *602 Squadron* and 34108 *Wincanton.* On departing from these Southern locos another link in the steam chain was snapped forever.

Further trips in May and June to various parts of the country was

'Britannia' Class 4-6-2 No 70015 Apollo *in reserve at 12B Carlisle (Upperby). 2 July 1967*

'Flying Pig' 2-6-0 No 43137 outside the roundhouse at 52F North Blyth. 5 July 1967

followed by a week long one to the North and Scotland, our accommodation being a two man tent.

We commenced the week at Crewe (South) where many locos had been brought out of store for the summer services and steam was plentiful. Moving on to Northwich we were trapped in a traffic jam caused by a carnival. Hundreds of people of all ages pranced by dressed as fairies and the like, and the procession seemed endless, the last thing we wanted on a mammoth spotting trip! Normally, Northwich is a quiet town and either the entire population was involved or the same lot kept coming round and back again several times. Having eventually got rid of this crocodile, we carried on with the serious business of shed bashing.

The following day, having progressed as far as Carlisle where we saw 103 steam on Kingmoor, we made for the border and Scotland where we had not been for three years. Steam-wise we were too late, the last of the Scottish steam had been withdrawn in early June. Although we saw a number of locos in store we only saw one steam engine in service 9F 2-10-0 No 92093 of Kingmoor at Motherwell.

In the early hours of the fifth day we were near to Berwick and having considerable trouble finding ourselves a suitable camping spot. At one stage I nearly drove over a cliff up a lonely road, but returning to the A1 we eventually found a haven for the night on a grass verge. Having pitched the tent we settled down only to be disturbed by a rumbling sound which increased and the ground started to shake. Shooting out of the tent we found ourselves over the top of Cockburnspath tunnel on the East Coast main line. What a spot to choose!

Class J27 0-6-0 No 65882 inside one of the roundhouses at 52H Tyne Dock. This depot was one of the most derelict, yet it remained open and housed steam until September 1967. 5 July 1967

Shadows lengthen at 12A Carlisle Kingmoor, this once mighty steam shed being only three weeks off closure. (l. to r.) 8F 2-8-0 No 48192. 'Britannia' 4-6-2 No 70011 Hotspur *and Class 5 4-6-0 No 45236. Shed closure resulted in the withdrawal of all but one of the remaining 'Britannias'. 10 December 1967*

Alongside 8F Springs Branch Wigan, was a dumping ground for steam locos, and numbers increased as the end of steam approached. Class 4 2-6-0 No 76079 is the centre piece, and now preserved at Steamport, Southport. 18 February 1968

During the day we progressed southwards and in the late evening were in York. We did the shed and as we drove through York were overtaken by a Morris Minor being driven in an erratic manner. It careered out of sight and as we rounded the next bend it was upside down on its roof. As we stopped our car a group of passengers from a bus got off and righted the Morris. Out of the semi-squashed and falling apart wreckage emerged a drunken Irishman who, spotting Baz and myself about to get back into our car, came after us and in a flash was sat in the back passenger seat. He said: "Get me out of here, anywhere will do. I'll make it worth your while." I was so dumbfounded I couldn't have started the car even if I had wanted to. The next thing we knew was that we were surrounded by police officers asking all sorts of questions. The Irishman then confessed that he was the driver of the crashed car and that he had tried to bribe us into taking him away. Instead the police took him away!

The remainder of the week passed without incident and we arrived home having travelled some 2,250 miles and seen 825 steam. During this trip I spotted my last steam locomotive an 8F 2-8-0 No 48550 at Rose Grove. Baz also finished his off after spotting a K2 2-6-0 on Blyth. From now on it was a question of concentrating on seeing steam for as long as we could before the end came.

We went to South Wales in August, and in September we recorded the most mileage we had ever done in a short space of time, 844 miles in thirty-six hours.The area covered was across to Norfolk back to London, from there through to Kent and back home through London again. One of the sheds visited, Finsbury Park, was the scene of a classic comedy.

There were four of us on this trip, Baz, myself and two friends, Colin and Mick. I went to see the foreman, the plan being to keep him talking whilst the others nipped smartly round the shed. I explained to him that I used to work on the railways, we chatted for a while and he decided to take me round the shed. By now it was too late to inform him that there were three others with me.

We were stood between two diesels, and I noticed Baz tip-toe across the front of the depot and so did the foreman. He said; "Who's that?", to which I replied: "I don't know". A couple of minutes later Mick repeated the manoeuvre in the opposite direction.This time the comment from the bemused foreman was: "Well, who was that other fellow? Are you sure you are on your own?" "Oh yes, of course", I replied. "They're nothing to do with me". The crunch came when Colin, under the impression I had obtained permission for all of us, brazenly walked past writing down numbers.

The foreman said to me, "What the b....... hell is going on? The place is full of them, I intend to deal with this". He turned on his heel and disappeared. I rounded my friends up and we took off for the exit as fast as possible. The car was parked within the shed grounds and as we rounded

BR 9F Class 2-10-0 No 92054 leaves 8C Speke Junction for freight duty a few weeks before closure and end of steam in Liverpool. 26 March 1968

Without the instrusion of the Type 2 diesel, No D7549, one could be forgiven for thinking this scene at 9K Bolton was from the early 1960s. But in fact the photograph was taken only a few weeks before closure. (l. to r.) Class 5 4-6-0 Nos 45260, 44781 and 44929 and 8F 2-8-0 No 48392. 12 May 1968

Class 5 4-6-0 No 44802 pointing towards the coaling plant at 9K Bolton. 12 May 1968

the corner there to our horror we were confronted by the foreman who had locked the huge wrought iron gates, trapping us. Standing there with the key firmly in his grasp, he looked at me and said, "On your own, eh! What are you going to do about this then?" We were stumped. Once again fortune smiled on us, for he had a good sense of humour and after ticking us off unlocked the gate. At times, it must have been every bit as funny to these people as it was for us.

Stewarts Lane was a hard shed to bunk if on foot and was always guarded by a gate-keeper. Invariably they were of the P.P.O. ilk and always got the greatest pleasure out of refusing entry to railfans. By car it was easy as one simply drove past them, but Baz told me of an occasion when he and a couple of friends were refused entry. They noticed that at the back of the gatekeeper's hut there was a gap out of sight of the official. They hid round the corner for a while, returned and made their way round the back of the hut. All went well to start with but the gap narrowed and was strewn with brooms, shovels and other hazards. With the rummaging, banging and stumbling over these obstacles, it came as no surprise that the gatekeeper was waiting for them as they emerged.

Class 8F 2-8-0 No 48338 and Class 5 4-6-0 No 73069 at 9H Patricroft shed. 12 May 1968

Only two weeks from closure at 9H Patricroft with Class 5 4-6-0 No 45156 Ayrshire Yeomanry *in steam, and Class 5 4-6-0 No 45287. 22 June 1968*

Three active Class 5 4-6-0s in the yard at 9D Newton Heath only two weeks before closure. (l. to r.) Nos 45200, 45096, and 44949. 22 June 1968

During September the four of us went up North, and arriving at our first point of call we drove in past the apparently empty gatekeeper's hut and boldly parked alongside the shed. As we emerged from the car and nonchalantly made our way towards the entrance a great voice boomed out behind us, "OI, WHERE DO YOU THINK YORE GOING?" I glanced round and noticed the man was not wearing the familiar coat of a foreman/shedmaster nor the bowler or trilby of an inspector, and I motioned to my companions to ignore him and carry on. A second repeated bellowing was enough to put the others off and they stopped and turned back. Unaware of this I carried on, but the third bellow was even louder than the others put together. "OI, ARE YOU DEAF?, YES YOU, BIGHEAD!, COME HERE!" Realising I was on my own and that he was directing his remarks at me I scampered back to my mates.

The owner of the voice looked large even from a distance, and the nearer we got to him the bigger he seemed to grow. Standing there, hands on hips, he was well over six feet tall and almost as wide, with a nasty looking face. "WELL", he said, "WHERE DO YOU THINK YORE WERE GOING?", he menacingly repeated. We tried to explain that we had been on our way to ask the foreman for permission to go round the depot, a fact he totally ignored.

While all this was going on, a small wizened fellow approached from the direction of the gatekeeper's hut, yet another out of the P.P.O. mould. He was the complete opposite to the other man, under five feet tall, thin as a rake and the classic example of one bullied at school who would take it out on anyone he could in later years.

An immaculate Class 5 4-6-0 No 45017 in steam at Carnforth. This shed with Lostock Hall and Rose Grove were the last three steam sheds in Britain. 27 July 1968

Two survivors inside Carnforth shed. Class 5 and Class 4 4-6-0s Nos 73069 and 75027, the latter being preserved on the Bluebell Railway. 27 July 1968

Two 8F 2-8-0s in store at 10D Lostock Hall. (l. to r.) Nos 48293 and 48546. 30 July 1968

Seen standing side by side they presented a funny sight, 'The Giant and the Dwarf' and we nicknamed them Bluto and Mr. Magoo. Everything the big man said was repeated by the other — "DO YOU NORE YORE TRESPASSING?" — "Aye, do you nore yore trespassing?" —"YOU DROVE STRAIGHT PAST GATEKEEPER", — "Aye, I'm the gatekeeper", — "WHY DIDN'T YOU STOP AT GATE?, THAT'S WHAT IT'S THERE FOR", —"Aye, you should have stopped, because I'm the gatekeeper", — "I OUGHT TO CALL POLICE", —"Aye, call the police" and so it went on. If the situation had not been so potentially dangerous we would have collapsed laughing. Eventually he said — "YOU OUGHT TO BE ARRESTED FOR TRESPASSING, GET OUT OF HERE AND DON'T LET ME SEE YOU HERE AGAIN". At long last we were able to escape; it hadn't been much fun cowering there wondering what the devil he was going to do. Unfortunately we were destined to meet him again!

At the beginning of November I went to Crewe (South), now closed, its fifty steam locos gaunt and silent. A few days later Manchester was visited, followed in early December by a trip to Liverpool and Carlisle. It was to be our last visit to the mighty Kingmoor as a steam centre and was completed despite an ominous warning by a railwayman: "You shouldn't be in here, you know. You can count yourself lucky that the dog handler has gone to Upperby". We chose to ignore him, but all the same kept a close watch.

Although still well populated, many of the sixty-eight steam locos were stored and its once proud fleet of "Britannias" were reduced to a mere handful with only six as working examples. The shed was due to close at the end of the month and we felt very sad on leaving as it had offered us many challenges and much pleasure since 1962.

Thus the year of 1967 ended on a low note and the immediate future for steam looked bleaker than it had ever done.

Patricroft shed visited for the last time with BR Class 5 4-6-0 No 73143 stripped of its main coupling rods. These Caprotti locos were for many years the mainstay of expresses to North Wales. 30 July 1968

1968

So this was finally to be the last year: BR announced that steam would finish by August with Carnforth, Lostock Hall and Rose Grove being the very last steam sheds. The situation in January was that apart from these three sheds, Bolton, Buxton, Edge Hill, Heaton Mersey, Newton Heath, Patricroft, Speke, Stockport and Trafford Park were still open as steam depots, but not for much longer.

Our first trip of the year was to the London sheds and our progress was hampered by bad weather and running out of petrol en route. Consequently, by the time we arrived at our last shed, Stratford, it was late in the evening and halfway round the depot we were apprehended by two plain-clothed policemen attracted to us by the fact that Mick had been standing in the centre of a well lit yard. After explaining our reasons for being there they seemed satisfied we were not thieves or vandals, but insisted on escorting us out, lecturing us on the dangers of trespassing in busy depots. One of them even went as far as to point to the front of a diesel and say, "Look at the blood on there, that was caused by one of your lot". It was plaintively obvious it had been caused by a bird and I nearly pointed out that it was not often anybody came across a fourteen foot tall trainspotter but decided that discretion was the better part of valour.

Preserved Class A4 4-6-2 No 4498 (60007) Sir Nigel Gresley *prepared for eviction from 5B Crewe (South). In steam it made its way to Philadelphia, Co. Durham and a new home. 30 July 1968*

View of the yard at 10D Lostock Hall from the tender of BR Class 5 4-6-0 No 73069. Many of the locos were being prepared for farewell specials. 4 August 1968

Cleaned for farewell specials Class 5 4-6-0 No 45305 (now preserved) and Class 8F 2-8-0 No 48476 at 10D Lostock Hall. 4 August 1968

From February to May we had many visits to the remaining steam sheds, as well as to many others. For two weeks in early June, Baz, myself and Mick, did a massive trip over England, Wales and Scotland, and in terms of mileage it put all others in the shade — 3250 miles in which we saw 417 steam with nearly 2,500 diesels and electrics. It really came home to us during the course of this holiday just how quickly steam had disappeared off BR metals. There were a number of amusing incidents to look back on.

On the first day, for instance, whilst going round Cardiff (Canton) in the dark, Mick once again decided to do his trainspotting in the middle of a well-lit yard, this time outside the foreman's office, resulting in eviction for him, although we were not noticed. Later on we camped at Undy, near Severn Tunnel Junction. It was early in the morning and there was a heavy mist as we pitched our tent. We woke in the morning to find the fog had cleared, but found we had camped on a village green by a row of houses a short distance from a nearby bus-stop. A queue of people looked at us with bemused smiles as we emerged from the tent.

As we progressed it became more apparent that Mick was not only slapdash going round sheds but he was accident prone as well, tripping over all manner of things. This also threatened our activities inside sheds because of the noise he made and I often said to him "If you don't watch out you will have a real accident," which he always scoffed at.

Class 8F 2-8-0 No 48773 in steam at 10F Rose Grove prior to making its way to the Severn Valley Railway and active preservation. 4 August 1968

Class 5 4-6-0 No 45110 leaves Rainhill for Manchester on the leg from Liverpool of a BR 'Farewell to Steam' special. Now preserved on the Severn Valley Railway. 11 August 1968

Class 5 4-6-0s Nos 44871 and 44781 approaching Dent on the Carlisle-Manchester section of the BR 'Farewell to Steam' special. No 44781 was later used in the film the 'Virgin Soldiers' and later scrapped. No 44871 is preserved at Steamtown Carnforth. 11 August 1968

Sure enough he was soon to meet his Waterloo. We arrived at West Hartlepool shed in the early hours of a Sunday morning to find the depot in total darkness with the exception of one light above the office. Despite the presence of many diesels in the yard, the place was deathly silent and we had to creep around as quietly as possible. I had been into the second roundhouse and noted the numbers of the few locos there when Mick followed and, despite whispering that I had all the numbers, he brushed past me.

I looked at Baz and said, "What can you do with the bloke?", when there was an almighty crash and a scream loud enough to wake the dead. I almost jumped out of my skin and Baz promptly disappeared into hiding. The hideous scream seemed to go on for ever, echoing round the empty vastness of the shed. We expected the office door to burst open (we heard the sound of a large bolt being drawn) but as no-one emerged the occupant had obviously *locked himself in!*

LMS Class 5 4-6-0s Nos 45095, 45025 and 44874 in and around the ash plant and coaling plant at 10A Carnforth. 22 June 1968.

Baz and I got together and wondered what we would find. The screams from the pit had ceased, being replaced by softer moans and groans. What if he was badly injured? An ambulance and the police would have to be called and we would almost certainly be arrested. We found Mick, with the aid of a torch. In his haste he had trodden on some loose slates which had fallen with him into an inspection pit. He was more shocked than anything, and at the sight of him grovelling around on all fours in patches of oil muttering, "I can't find my pen," Baz and I collapsed into hysterics. We rescued him and his pen, and returned to the car as fast as possible.

At Sunderland, the shed was again in total darkness and on passing an outside building I peeped through a window and looked straight into the opening eyes of an awakening railwayman, I don't know who was more shocked, him or me. The next thing three or four of them hurtled through the door demanding to know what was going on. Bearing in mind that at this hour of the morning the excuse of looking for the foreman's office was a little lame, we were flabbergasted when they put the shed lights on and gave us a conducted tour.

We moved on and spent several fruitful days in Scotland, returning down the west coast of England, calling in at numerous steam sheds on the way. One of these just happened to be where we had encountered our friends *Bluto* and *Mr. Magoo* the previous September. However, we thought we would try our luck, hoping that lightning wouldn't strike twice in the same place.

We ensured that the gatekeeper's hut was empty before driving in and parking. Once over the footbridge we were away, but not for long, as we were soon apprehended by an official. Our ready-made excuse was that, having arrived earlier, we had seen a group of spotters waiting at the official entrance and, being a Sunday, we had assumed that there would be a guided tour in the afternoon. We had gone for a drink and on our return they had left. We assumed they were inside and, by using a short cut, had hoped to join them.

Trusty steed! The Ford motor car which did sterling service on the author's marathon tours, including the "Twelve Counties Tour" which covered 625 miles and seventeen sheds. Earlswood 1965.

Camped over the top of Cockburnspath Tunnel on the East Coast main line. What a place to choose! 5 July 1967.

Roughing it trainspotting style. "Baz" Homer (extreme left) and another enthusiast near Tebay on the West Coast main line. 2 July 1967.

It was important that the official should believe our story, which he did, hook, line and sinker. He said, "No lads, there's no visit today, I'll just check with main gate", which he did. Speaking to the gateman, he said, "I've got three well-dressed intelligent lads here who seem to think there's a visit on today". The answer was in the negative and he ended up *apologising to us*. "We have to be on our guard because many spotters try to get round unofficially, but not lads like you who have made a genuine mistake".

He let us out of a side gate and said we would have to make our own way back to the car. We thanked him and said our goodbyes, then once outside the gate were in the act of congratulating ourselves when a large familiar shape loomed towards us, it was *Bluto* himself. We couldn't believe our own eyes and considering our first meeting had not been so very long ago, we were surprised when he didn't recognise us.

"WHERE DO YOU THINK YORE GOING?", "DON'T YOU NORE YORE TRESPASSING?" and "I OUGHT TO CALL THE POLICE", all of these set-pieces were rattled out again, but at least the wretched gatekeeper was not with him this time. It didn't matter what reasons we had, he was again not prepared to listen and so it went on, ending with the now familiar phrase, "GET OUT BEFORE I CALL THE POLICE". This we did, and thankfully we never saw him again.

If we thought Mick had been a disaster at West Hartlepool, our next trip with him turned out even worse. It was to Derby in July. Baz and I needed only a handful of diesels and after parking on waste ground at the side of the works we nipped through a convenient hole in the wall, scooted swiftly round and back out to the car in a short space of time. Not for Mick, though; he insisted on laboriously writing down every number whether he needed to or not and fell further and further behind us.

Back in the car, time passed with no sign of Mick. It was a miserable, drizzle-laden day with poor visibility through heavy mist. Time ticked interminably on when Baz casually said, "Here comes Mick with a copper". I looked; and sure enough out of the mist and gloom emerged Mick and the long arm of the law. Mick was soaked; he had been caught inside the works by a British Transport policeman.

As we were on waste land I failed to see what the policeman could do to Baz and myself and after denying we had been there he leaned through our car window, rain cascading off his helmet and said, "I must warn you that anything you say will be taken down as evidence." We couldn't believe our ears. He took our details and said we would probably be prosecuted. We were not, but came very close to it and received a stern warning in writing.

At the end of July I twice visited the three remaining steam depots at

Carnforth, Lostock Hall and Rose Grove. Sunday 4 August was the last official day of steam and we went to Lostock Hall and Rose Grove. At the former depot many of the surviving locos were being cleaned for rail tours and some were fitted with old original shed plates eg. 27C Southport.

My records show the following engines in steam Nos 44781, 44871, 44874, 44888, 44894, 45017, 45073, 45110, 45260, 45287, 45305, 45318, 45407, 48340, 48476, 48493, 70013 *Oliver Cromwell* and 73069. We reluctantly moved on to Rose Grove where we found only three locos in steam No 48519 on a nearby freight with Nos 48348 and 48773 in the shed yard.

Sunday 11 August was the final one for steam with a special train from Liverpool to Carlisle via Manchester. Four different locos were used Nos 44781/871 double-headed with Nos 45110 and "Britannia" No 70013 *Oliver Cromwell* used separately on different legs. We saw No 45110 at Rainhill and No 70013 *Oliver Cromwell* at Ais Gill. At the latter location I doubt if the local inhabitants had ever seen before or since the enormous numbers of cars and coaches which gathered there on this particular day.

At Ribblehead Viaduct we had a final glimpse of the train behind Nos 44781/871 as it disappeared into railway history; and true to his past form Baz leapt out of the car and into a waterlogged ditch! It was so hard to believe that the long road we had travelled with steam had finally come to an end. In these action packed twelve years I had spotted in excess of 12,000 individual steam locomotives.

The appropriate ending for this story comes in the words of a chart topping song from 1968 — 'Those Were The Days My Friend — We Thought They'd Never End . . .'

Ex-LMS Class 8F 2-8-0 No 48773 at 10F Rose Grove awaiting removal to the Severn Valley Railway for preservation. The yellow cabside stripe indicates that the loco was not permitted to run under wires on electrified lines. 4 August 1968.

Postscript

Chasing Steam on Shed has taken me on a wonderful journey back in time. I hope that you, the reader, have likewise enjoyed being with me and my mates, Baz, Lanks, Mick and Colin, and that you have identified with some of our hilarious shed bunks, and shared in our elation and disappointments.

For many of you our exploits will have no doubt brought back memories of similar youthful escapades, and in that respect we are bloodbrothers in our love of the steam locomotive.

What began as a child's pastime has given me untold pleasures and rewards. My journeyings by road and rail in pursuit of steam have done wonders for my knowledge of the topography and geography of the United Kingdom. It has also taught me to value good companionship; and my face-to-face confrontation with persons in authority has certainly given me a unique insight into the complexities of human nature.

When I look back on it all, I realise how lenient and understanding most of the shedmasters, gatekeepers and yard foremen were in dealing with us pestering shed bashers.

But although we were a nuisance, perhaps more of an irritant, and at times could technically have been breaking the law of trespass we were never bent on doing harm or creating havoc.

After that bleak day back in August 1968 when BR finally killed off steam, there was a void in my life which I thought would be very difficult to fill. It was then I sat down and began to check and cross-check through my many notebooks and records of shed visits and loco spotting.

Unwittingly I had started on the mammoth task of documenting the movements of every single one of the 18,000 or so locomotives which ran under British Railway's ownership from January 1957 until their demise in August 1968.

Seven years of unremitting research and writing were brought to fruition with the publication of the first volume of the "What Happened to Steam" series of booklets, and there is still a long way to go before the final volume, Number 50, comes off the press.

Of course, there were many who thought the end of steam would see the hobby interest fall away, but thanks to preservation societies and their hardworking volunteers we now have an abundance of steam locos to go and see. And, of course, the jewel in BRs crown: the lifting of the steam ban and the running of a regular programme of steam specials.

Might I end on a cautionary note, by entreating all steam lovers to support a steam preservation society in some way or another; please do book your seat on a steam special. Do it this year, not next. One day it will be too late. Steam, even in aspic, cannot last forever.

Ex-LMS Class 8F 2-8-0 No 48191 in the yard at 10F Rose Grove. Many of these hard-working freight locos saw service overseas during the 1939-1945 war, and a number are still in service in Turkey. 12 May 1968.

Locomotive Depots 1957

1A Willesden
1B Camden
1C Watford
1D Devons Road (Bow)
1E Bletchley
Leighton Buzzard

2A Rugby
Seaton
2B Nuneaton
2C Warwick
2D Coventry
2E Northampton
2F Market Harborough

3A Bescot
3B Bushbury
3C Walsall
3D Aston
3E Monument Lane

5A Crewe (North)
Whitchurch
5B Crewe (South)
Gresty Lane
5C Stafford
5D Stoke
5E Alsager
5F Uttoxeter

6A Chester
6B Mold Junction
6C Birkenhead
6D Chester (Northgate)
6E Wrexham
6F Bidston
6G Llandudno Junction
6H Bangor
6J Holyhead
6K Rhyl

8A Edge Hill (Liverpool)
8B Warrington
8C Speke Junction
8D Widnes
8E Brunswick (Liverpool)

9A Longsight (Manchester)
9B Stockport
9C Macclesfield
9D Buxton
9E Northwich

10A Springs Branch Wigan
10B Preston
10C Patricroft
10D Sutton Oak

11A Carnforth
11B Barrow
Coniston
11C Oxenholme
11D Tebay

12A Carlisle (Upperby)
12B Penrith
12C Workington

14A Cricklewood
14B Kentish Town
14C St. Albans

15A Wellingborough
15B Kettering
15C Leicester (Midland)
15D Bedford

16A Nottingham
16B Kirkby
16C Mansfield

17A Derby
17B Burton
Horninglow
Overseal
17C Coalville
17D Rowsley
Cromford
Middleton
Sheep Pasture
17E Heaton Mersey
17F Trafford Park

18A Toton
18B Westhouses
18C Hasland
18D Staveley (Barrow Hill)
Sheepbridge

19A Sheffield (Grimesthorpe)
19B Millhouses
19C Canklow

21A Saltley
21B Bournville
21C Bromsgrove

22A Bristol (Barrow Road)
22B Gloucester (Barnwood)
Dursley
Tewkesbury

24A Accrington
24B Rose Grove
24C Lostock Hall
24D Lower Darwen
24E Blackpool (South)
Blackpool (North)
24F Fleetwood
24G Skipton
24H Hellifield
24J Lancaster (Green Ayre)

26A Newton Heath
26B Agecroft
26C Bolton
26D Bury
26E Lees

27A Bank Hall
27B Aintree
27C Southport
27D Wigan (L & Y)
27E Walton

30A Stratford
Brentwood
Chelmsford
Enfield Town
Epping
Ilford
Wood Street
30B Hertford East
Buntingford
Ware
30C Bishops Stortford
30E Colchester
Braintree
Clacton
Maldon
Walton-on-Naze
30F Parkeston

31A Cambridge
Ely
Huntingdon East
Saffron Waldron
31B March
Wisbech
31C Kings Lynn
Hunstanton
31D South Lynn
31E Bury St. Edmunds
Sudbury

32A Norwich
Cromer Beach
Dereham
Swaffham
Wymondham

32B Ipswich
Felixtowe Town
Stowmarket
32C Lowestoft Central
32D Yarmouth South Town
32E Yarmouth Vauxhall
32F Yarmouth Beach
32G Melton Constable
Norwich City

33A Plaistow
33B Tilbury
33C Shoeburyness

34A Kings Cross

34B Hornsey
34C Hatfield
34D Hitchin
34E Neasden
Aylesbury
Chesham

35A New England
Spalding
Stamford
35B Grantham
35C Peterborough (Spital Bridge)

36A Doncaster
36B Mexborough
Wath
36C Frodingham
36D Barnsley
36E Retford
Newark

38A Colwick
38B Annesley
38C Leicester G.C.
38D Staveley G.C.
38E Woodford Halse

39A Gorton
Dinting
Hayfield

40A Lincoln
Lincoln (St. Marks)
40B Immingham
Grimsby
New Holland
40D Tuxford
40E Langwith Junction
40F Boston
Sleaford

41A Darnall (Sheffield)

50A York
50B Leeds (Neville Hill)
50C Selby
50D Starbeck
50E Scarborough
50F Malton
Pickering
50G Whitby

51A Darlington
Middleton-on-Teesdale
51B Newport
51C West Hartlepool
51D Middlesbrough
51E Stockton
51F West Auckland
51G Haverton Hill
51H Kirby Stephen
51J Northallerton
51K Saltburn

52A Gateshead
Bowes Bridge
52B Heaton
52C Blaydon
Alston
Hexham
52D Tweedmouth
Alnmouth
52E Percy Main
52F North Blyth
South Blyth

53A Hull (Dairycoates)
53B Hull (Botanic Gardens)
53C Hull (Springhead)
Alexandra Dock
53D Bridlington
53E Goole

54A Sunderland
Durham
54B Tyne Dock
54C Borough Gardens
54D Consett

55A Leeds (Holbeck)
55B Stourton
55C Farnley Junction
55D Royston
55E Normanton
55F Manningham
55G Huddersfield

56A Wakefield
56B Ardsley
56C Copley Hill
56D Mirfield
56E Sowerby Bridge
56F Low Moor
56G Bradford (H. St.)

60A Inverness
Dingwall
Kyle of Lochalsh
60B Aviemore
Boat of Garten
60C Helmsdale
Dornoch
Tain
60D Wick
Thurso
60E Forres

61A Kittybrewster
Ballater
Fraserburgh
Inverurie
Peterhead
61B Ferryhill (Aberdeen)
61C Keith
Banff
Elgin

62A Thornton Junction
Anstruther
Burntisland
Ladybank
Methil
62B Dundee (Tay Bridge)
Arbroath
Dundee West
Montrose
St. Andrews
62C Dunfermline
Alloa

63A Perth
Aberfeldy
Crieff
63B Stirling
Killin
63C Forfar
63D Oban
Ballachulish

64A St. Margarets (Edinburgh)
Dunbar
Galashiels
Longniddry
North Berwick
64B Haymarket
64C Dalry Road
64D Carstairs
64E Polmont
64F Bathgate
64G Hawick
Riccarton
St. Boswells

65A Eastfield (Glasgow)
Arrochar
65B St. Rollox
65C Parkhead
65D Dawsholm
Dumbarton
65E Kipps
65F Grangemouth
65G Yoker
65H Helensburgh
65I Balloch
65J Fort William
Mallaig

66A Polmadie (Glasgow)
66B Motherwell
66C Hamilton
66D Greenock (Ladyburn)
Greenock (Pr. P)

67A Corkerhill (Glasgow)
67B Hurlford
Beith
Muirkirk
67C Ayr
67D Adrossan

68A Carlisle (Kingmoor)
68B Dumfries
68C Stranraer
Newton Stewart
68D Beattock

68E	Carlisle (Canal)
70A	Nine Elms
70B	Feltham
70C	Guildford
70D	Basingstoke
70E	Reading (South)
70F	Fratton
70G	Newport Isle- of-Wight
70H	Ryde Isle-of-Wight
71A	Eastleigh
	Andover Junction
	Lymington
	Winchester
71B	Bournemouth
	Branksome
71G	Bath Green Park
	Radstock
71H	Templecombe
71I	Southampton
	Docks
71J	Highbridge
72A	Exmouth Junction
	Bude
	Exmouth
	Lyme Regis
	Okehampton
	Seaton
72B	Salisbury
72C	Yeovil
72D	Plymouth (Friary)
	Callington
72E	Barnstaple Junction
	Ilfracombe
	Torrington
72F	Wadebridge
73A	Stewarts Lane
73B	Bricklayers Arms
73C	Hither Green
73D	Gillingham
73E	Faversham
74A	Ashford
74B	Ramsgate
74C	Dover
	Folkestone
74D	Tonbridge
74E	St. Leonards
75A	Brighton
75B	Redhill
75C	Norwood Junction
75D	Horsham
75E	Three Bridges
75F	Tunbridge Wells West
81A	Old Oak Common
81B	Slough
	Marlow
81C	Southall
81D	Reading
	Henley-on-Thames
81E	Didcot
81F	Oxford
	Fairford
82A	Bristol (Bath Road)
	Bath
	Wells
	Weston
	Yatton
82B	St. Phillips Marsh
82C	Swindon
	Chippenham
82D	Westbury
	Frome
82E	Yeovil
82F	Weymouth
	Bridport
83A	Newton Abbot
	Ashburton
	Kingsbridge
83B	Taunton
	Bridgwater
83C	Exeter (St. Davids)
	Tiverton Junction
83D	Laira (Plymouth)
	Launceston
83E	St. Blazey
	Bodmin
	Moorswater
83F	Truro
83G	Penzance
	St. Ives
	Helston
84A	Wolverhampton
	(Stafford Road)
84B	Oxley
84C	Banbury
84D	Leamington
84E	Tyseley
	Stratford
84F	Stourbridge
84G	Shrewsbury
	Builth Road
	Clee Hill
	Craven Arms
	Knighton
84H	Wellington (Salop)
84J	Croes Newydd
	Bala
	Penmaenpool
	Trawsfynydd
84K	Chester (G.W.R.)
85A	Worcester
	Evesham
	Kingham
85B	Gloucester
	Brimscombe
	Cheltenham
	Cirencester
	Lydney
	Tetbury
85C	Hereford
	Ledbury
	Leominster
	Ross
85D	Kidderminster
86A	Newport (Ebbw Junction)
86B	Newport Pill
86C	Cardiff (Canton)
86D	Llantrisant
86E	Severn Tunnel Junction
86F	Tondu
86G	Pontypool Road
	Abergavenny
86H	Aberbeeg
86J	Aberdare
86K	Tredegar
87A	Neath
	Glyn Neath
	Neath (N & B)
87B	Duffryn Yard
87C	Danygraig
87D	Swansea East Dock
87E	Landore
87F	Llanelly
	Burry Port
	Pantyffynon
87G	Carmarthen
87H	Neyland
	Cardigan
	Milford Haven
	Pembroke Dock
	Whitland
87J	Goodwick
87K	Swansea Victoria
	Gurnos
	Llandovery
	Upper Bank
88A	Cardiff Cathays
	Radyr
88B	Cardiff East Dock
88C	Barry
88D	Merthyr
	Cae Harris
	Dowlais Central
	Rhymney
88E	Abercynon
88F	Treherbert
	Ferndale
89A	Oswestry
	Llanidloes
	Moat Lane
89B	Brecon
	Builth Wells
89C	Machynlleth
	Aberayron
	Aberystwyth
	Aberystwyth V of R
	Portmadoc
	Pwllheli

"What Happened to Steam" series

—COMMENCED APRIL/MAY 1980

Volume 1 — G.W.R. 2-8-0's—28xx, 38xx & 47xx series (26 pages).
Volume 2 — G.W.R. 'Castles & Kings' (30 pages).
Volume 3 — L.M.S. 'Jubilee's' (30 pages).
Volume 4 — L.N.E.R. A4, A3, A1 & A2 Pacifics (30 pages).
Volume 5 — S.R. 'West Country/Battle of Britain', 'Merchant Navy' and 'Schools' classes (30 pages).
Volume 6 — G.W.R. 'Halls' (34 pages).
Volume 7 — L.M.S. 'Patriot', 'Royal Scot', 'Princess' & 'Coronation' classes (30 pages).
Volume 8 — L.N.E.R. V2 Class 2-6-2's Nos. 60800-983 (26 pages).
Volume 9 — B.R. 'Britannia's', 'Duke', 'Clans' and Class 5 4-6-0's (34 pages).
Volume 10 — G.W.R. 'Counties', 'Granges', 'Modified Halls' & 'Manors' (34 pages).
Volume 11 — S.R. 4-6-0's — H15, S15, 'King Arthur' & 'Lord Nelson' classes. G16 4-8-0 Tanks & H16 4-6-2 Tanks (26 pages).
Volume 12 — B.R. 9F 2-10-0's Nos. 92000-251 (34 pages).
Volume 13 — L.N.E.R. B1 Class 4-6-0's Nos. 61000-409 (54 pages).
Volume 14 — G.W.R. 2-6-0's — 43xx, 53xx, 63xx & 73xx/93xx series. Dukedog 4-4-0's (30 pages).
Volume 15 — L.M.S. Ivatt 2-6-0's Nos. 43000-161 & 46400-527 (42 pages).
Volume 16 — S.R. 2-6-0's — K, N, N1, U & U1 classes. W Class 2-6-4 Tanks (30 pages).
Volume 17 — B.R. Class 4 4-6-0's & Class 4 2-6-0's Nos. 75000-79 & 76000-114 (30 pages).
Volume 18 — L.N.E.R. 4-6-0's — B16, B12 & B2/B17 Classes (26 pages).
Volume 19 — L.M.S. 'Crab' & 'Stanier Crab' 2-6-0's Nos. 42700-944 & 42945-84 (42 pages).
Volume 20 — G.W.R. small wheeled 2-6-2 Tanks — 45xx & 55xx series. 14xx/58xx series 0-4-2 Tanks (30 pages).
Volume 21 — B.R. Classes — 77xxx, 78xxx, 80xxx, 82xxx & 84xxx series (46 pages).
Volume 22 — G.W.R. 2-6-2 Tanks — 31xx, 41xx, 51xx, 61xx & 81xx series (34 pages).
Volume 23 — L.M.S. Class 5 4-6-0's Nos. 44658-45499 (106 pages).
Volume 24 — L.N.E.R. 2-6-0's — K2, K3/K5 & K1/K4 Classes (46 pages).

Volume 25 — S.R. 0-6-0's — C, C2X, 01, Q, Q1, 700 & 0395 Classes. S.R. 4-4-0's — D1, E1, L, L1 & T9 Classes (42 pages).
Volume 26 — W.D. 2-8-0's Nos. 90000-732 & 2-10-0's Nos. 90750-74 (94 pages)
Volume 27 — G.W.R. 57xx Pannier Tank 0-6-0's — 36xx, 46xx, 57xx, 67xx, 77xx, 87xx & 96xx series (94 pages).
Volume 28 — L.M.S. 8F 2-8-0's Nos. 48000-775 and the S. & D. 2-8-0's Nos. 53800-10. (86 pages). —Available May 1982.
Volume 29 — L.N.E.R. 4-4-0's — D30, D34, D16, D11 & D49 Classes. — Available June 1982.
Volume 30 — S.R. Tank Engines — Classes B4, USA, G6, R1, P, E2, A1X, E1/R, E3, E4, E4X, E6, E6X, M7, 02, H, 0298, Z & 0415. — Available June 1982.

The prices of these books varies between 75 pence and £3 depending on the size of classes and numbers of pages involved. If interested in this series please send an SAE to — P. B. Hands, 190 Yoxall Road, Shirley, Solihull, West Midlands, B90 3RN.

The author alongside the preserved remains of "Castle" Class 4-6-0 No 5080 Defiant *at Birmingham Railway Museum, Tyseley.*

FINIS!

Ex-LMS workhorse Class 5 4-6-0 No 44829 cut-up on site at 9K Bolton. 27 July 1968.